YA 523.1 S796
Startalk :everything you ever need to
know about space travel, sci-fi

WITHDRAWN

STARTALK

With Neil deGrasse Tyson

Everything You Ever Need to Know About Space Travel, Sci-Fi, the Human Race, the Universe, and Beyond

Young Readers Edition

NATIONAL
GEOGRAPHIC

WASHINGTON, D.C.

To all the fans of *StarTalk,*
whose insatiable appetite for science has inspired
the rich buffet on which this book is based

StarTalk and its associated television, radio, podcast, and other media broadcasts
are intended for mature audiences and may not be suitable for all audiences.
Viewer and listener discretion is advised.

> *"Our universe is filled with secrets and mysteries, leaving us with many questions to be answered. We find ourselves searching for those answers as the very fabric of space, science, and society are converging. Here, for the first time, these worlds collide!"*
> —*STARTALK RADIO* INTRODUCTION

Introduction

With those words, and the support of the National Science Foundation (NSF), the first broadcast of *StarTalk Radio* beamed out in 2007 across all of space and time. What has followed—on the radio, on the Internet, and on the National Geographic Channel—is now a movement that has thrown science and pop culture together into a whirling singularity and hurled the result out into our universe for all to enjoy.

Conversations on StarTalk can delve into viruses, like HIV, and medical advances.

If you're new to *StarTalk,* you may be wondering: What am I getting into? The millions of fans out there have, no doubt, millions of answers to this very good question. Maybe you can get a sense from real data. In a survey of three arbitrarily chosen *StarTalk* audience members, we've obtained these three assessments:

1. *"StarTalk* is a fun show with an intellectual science bent."
2. *"StarTalk* is a discussion of pop culture within the context of science."
3. *"StarTalk* is a way where you can learn science-y stuff through non-science-y stuff—and it's funny!"

What is *StarTalk*? The name says it all: Stars talk. Movie stars. TV stars. Comedy stars. Stars of all other kinds, as well—artists, activists, authors, opinion shapers, policymakers, and, of course, scientists. Sometimes, the talk is about stars, like the kind that

Astrophysicist Neil deGrasse Tyson hosts the StarTalk radio and television talk shows.

On StarTalk, *Neil and guest stars discuss all matters of the universe.*

have nuclear fusion in their cores and whose light twinkles as it passes through our atmosphere. Mostly, though, it's about anything and everything under those stars; and it's not an interview or a publicity piece—it's a conversation. *StarTalk* has celebrity, and comedy, and crazy egg-headed science. In a world where compartmentalization is increasingly the norm, such seemingly disparate elements, at first glance, would seem hard to combine. *StarTalk* reminds us all that they're not in the least disparate; not only do they play nice together, they've always been peas in a pod—we all just forget that sometimes. On *StarTalk,* science and society link arms and do-si-do in a spirited square dance of laughter and shared discovery. On *StarTalk,* everyone can love art, music, poetry, politics, engineering, science, and math all at the same time. Every pursuit and pursuer—be they scientifically thinking comedians or comedically thinking scientists, or anyone else—come together, inspired by the feeling of awe that comes from pondering the mysterious. Albert Einstein called that feeling "the source of all true art and science," and *StarTalk* is its embodiment—a joyous mind meld of all ways of thinking and being!

Find out what makes an aurora borealis light up the sky on page 85.

Now you hold in your hands the result of another mind meld: an evolution that happens when digital and print media collide. The skilled team at National Geographic Books has helped *StarTalk* jump from photons to paper, to bottle the lightning of the show's spirit and character into a package you can enjoy even if you've run out of battery power or aren't getting a wireless signal. On these pages—just like on the radio, podcasts, and television—stars talk. They're not "reported on," interviewed, or exposed, like they might be by a news show, magazine, or tabloid. We can see what they said and hear in our heads how they said it. Want to know why Stephen Colbert loves having scientists on his show? How Mayim Bialik feels about the world of *The Big Bang Theory*? Or what Dr. Neil deGrasse Tyson thinks about time travel, visiting Mars, or Superman's body temperature? It's all here on these pages, in their own words. On *StarTalk,* there is no "they." There is only "we." We are all invited to partake, unabashed and unafraid, without bias or judgment, in the interchange of ideas, imagination, and humanity's evidence-based understanding of our universe, our world, and ourselves. That's how science works.

Now get busy. Turn the page and discover what *StarTalk* is. Let's do this! And as Neil always says when he bids the audience farewell: Keep looking up. ∎

Spacecraft, like Soyuz, are always a hot topic—and StarTalk *gets real insight into them from astronauts.*

Satellites orbiting in space transmit signals—including StarTalk's*— to satellite dishes on Earth.*

About This Book

nside this book, we've taken the best of *StarTalk* from the airwaves to the page. You'll find the voices of guests who have appeared on the podcast and television show, including actors, comedians, politicians, astronauts, entrepreneurs, millionaires, physicists, neurologists, and biologists, just to name a few. We'll tackle questions that have led some of our greatest discussions on *StarTalk* over the years, and dive deeper into the science behind our universe. And we've got a whole lot of that universe to cover. This book is divided into four sections to make it easier for you to navigate your way through the world of *StarTalk:* "Space," "Planet Earth," "Being Human," and "Futures Imagined." Within these pages you'll discover the mystery behind black holes; real ideas for tackling climate change; just what makes us humans tick; and the amazing science behind science fiction. And there's a lot to take in. Just take a look at what these pages have on offer:

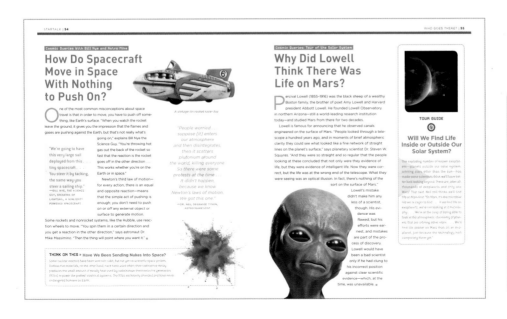

Love what you're reading and want more? We've made it easy for you. Look for the orange bar above the text: That's the name of the *StarTalk* episode this conversation came from. Go to star talkradio.net to hear more. And look to the green text for insightful quotes, or a deeper insight into the topic at hand.

StarTalk Live! Water World (Part 1)

Can I Drink Heavy Water?

Ordinary water has two hydrogen atoms and one oxygen atom: H_2O. The stuff we call heavy water has two deuterium atoms and one oxygen, and it's a little bit denser than ordinary water. Any water could have a tiny bit of heavy water in it, but to get a glass of it, you would have to start with a huge amount of water and extract the heavy water out.

Heavy water got a bad rap because of its use in developing nuclear weapons. Could you still drink it? Sure, says Neil. "You would slow down, though."

Comedian Eugene Mirman isn't buying it and asks, "Really? You wouldn't die?"

Not at all. Heavy water is made with deuterium atoms, which are actually hydrogen atoms with an extra neutron in each nucleus. So heavy water is practically identical to regular H_2O. It's not poisonous or anything. But it might not behave exactly the way you expect water to when you drink it.

Lab mice have had the experience, but we can only speculate what would happen to a human drinking heavy water. Judging by the numbers, though, heavy water is 11 percent more massive than a molecule of regular water, and two-thirds of your body mass is water—so after drinking heavy water, you would be just a little heavier.

Two glasses demonstrate the concept of heavy water and regular water

DID YOU KNOW
In every million gallons of seawater, there is about three ounces of naturally occurring heavy water.

THINK ON THIS ▸ How Much of Earth's Water Is Drinkable?

StarTalk Live! Water World (Parts 1 and 2)

Will World War III Be About Water?

Millions of people worldwide are forced to leave their homes each year because of water—either too much of it causing flooding, or too little of it causing drought and famine. "The Pentagon has done two assessments over the last decade," says Robert F. Kennedy, Jr., attorney and president of Waterkeeper Alliance, "and in both those assessments they've said that global warming, and particularly water shortages, are the principal threat to America's national security because of the disruption to global political systems and populations that it's going to cause."

High-stakes business investments come into play as well, continues Kennedy. "In the last 10 years, water privatization has become a trillion-dollar industry, according to the World Bank. We've already seen water wars fought all over the world—in Bolivia, in Cochabamba, and Belize, and many other countries where foreign companies have come in, privatized local water supplies, and then raised rates and literally killed poor people who can't afford those higher water rates."

Displaced and desperate people are much more likely to be part of civil and political strife, including crime and terrorism. Furthermore, many of the most politically sensitive places in the world, such as the Middle East, are in desert regions. Water issues can fuel violent conflict.

DID YOU KNOW
In sub-Saharan Africa, most people gather their water from wells, springs, lakes, and rivers. The time spent gathering water there totals 40 billion hours a year.

If only water wars could be fought with water guns.

"There are millions of environmental refugees every year, throughout the world, who are driven off their land and who are creating civil strife, and political strife, and security problems that affect the United States because of water shortages."
—ROBERT F. KENNEDY, JR., ATTORNEY AND PRESIDENT OF WATERKEEPER ALLIANCE

THINK ON THIS ▸ How Much Does That Bottle of Water Really Cost?

We jump deep into the topics on every page—but some of our best stuff comes from the hundreds of guests who have appeared on *StarTalk* over the years. The orange quotes throughout this book are the wise—and often hilarious—words of these stars. Use the "Did You Know" facts to impress your friends at trivia. The "Think on This" sidebars answer the initial question posed on the page, but from a different angle.

If in Space, No One Can Hear You Scream . . .

Why did we hear explosions in *Gravity*? Movies don't have to be scientifically accurate to be entertaining. *Star Wars*, one of the great sci-fi movie franchises of all time, is fundamentally untrue to the laws of physics, but we like it anyway. How about closer-to-Earth movies, like *The Martian*? Here are a few comments from Neil, many of them tweeted right after he saw the movie.

◀ **GRAVITATIONAL HAIRSTYLING**
@neiltyson: "Mysteries of #Gravity: Why [Sandra] Bullock's hair, in otherwise convincing zero-G scenes, did not float freely on her head? Must be using really good astronaut mousse."

▶ **BETTER TOGETHER**
@neiltyson: "Mysteries of #Gravity: When [George] Clooney releases Bullock's tether, he drifts away. In zero-G a single tug brings them together." But then where's the drama in that?"

◀ **WHAT'S IN A TITLE?**
@neiltyson: "Mysteries of #Gravity: Why Bullock, a medical Doctor, is servicing the Hubble Space Telescope"
@neiltyson: "Mysteries of #Gravity: Astronaut Clooney informs medical doctor Bullock what happens medically during oxygen deprivation."

◀ **SAY IT AIN'T SO!**
"Yes, absolutely, the sandstorm [in *The Martian*] is inaccurate . . . I just didn't care. I wanted a good reason to strand him there, and at the time I wrote it most people didn't know that." —Andy Weir, author of *The Martian*

▲ **MARTIAN GARDENING**
The Martian's greenhouse is full of potatoes? As long as there is enough water and grow lights, maybe. Essential soil nutrients for potato growth, though, are probably lacking, even with fertilizer.

◀ **SPACE TRAVELERS**
The rotating sections of *The Martian*'s spacecraft can indeed create acceleration that mimics gravity on a large spaceship. We still need some engineering innovations to make it possible, though.

▲ **STAR POWER**
@neiltyson: "In #StarWars #TheForceAwakens, if you were to suck all of a star's energy into your planet, your planet would vaporize." Bye-bye, Starkiller.

◀ **SPACE VOLUME**
@neiltyson: "In #StarWars #TheForceAwakens, the TIE fighters made exactly the same sound in the vacuum of space as in planetary atmospheres." Same goes for the X-wings and the Millennium Falcon.

Not all of these spreads come directly from the show—we've created collections in each of the sections in this book to expand your knowledge even more. Look to these pages for timelines of food in space, the history of apocalyptic theories, the real science behind sci-fi dramas, and much more.

There are a lot of other informative sidebars throughout this compendium—each with its own flavor. Here's a handy chart of sidebar icons to make it easier for you to navigate:

 Laugh Out Loud: This sidebar features some of the most hilarious quotes from our seriously funny guests.

 Tour Guide: Learn all you need to know about our universe—from space station bathrooms to super moons.

 Back to Basics: You may be scientifically literate, but that doesn't mean you know it all. This box explains harder-to-grasp concepts.

 Biography: We've highlighted remarkable scientists who have changed how we view our world.

 Conversation: One of the best parts of *StarTalk* is the banter that arises in the studio. Look for these witty back-and-forths in our "Conversation" sidebars.

 Neil Tweets: Neil is a prolific tweeter. And we've brought his social media feed to these pages with some of his best tweets.

SPACE

On a bright sunny day or an inky black night,
we all wonder sometimes: What's out there, out of sight?
Beyond Earth's friendly confines, an entire universe awaits
our exploration. But wait! We need to be ready before we
go; we need to know how to get there, how our bodies and
minds will take the journey, and what to expect when we
arrive. Plus, we want to enjoy ourselves, right? Mere survival
isn't the goal; we want to travel in style! After all,
who knows if we'll meet anyone along the way . . .

"Mars is a geologist's dream place, but even if you're just a tourist, it would be stunning, too. You know what I would do? I would not only look down, I would look up, and I would take a picture of Earth in the Martian sky."

—DR. NEIL DEGRASSE TYSON, ASTROPHYSICIST

CHAPTER ONE

What Do I Pack for Mars?

Cooped up in a space capsule for three years? Most of us have a hard time sitting in a car for three hours! That's what we'll have to do, though, to make it to our planetary neighbor, the red planet—Mars.

We'll have to bring a lot with us, too. Sure, Mars may have some of the things we humans need: Vast underground frozen oceans may provide water; mineral resources may provide materials for building and growing things. So what *doesn't* Mars have that we'll need?

Mars isn't our only destination, of course. What do we need for space travel? We're really packing for generations of humans in space, well beyond the familiar confines of low-Earth orbit. Can humans handle living in space? We already have been—astronauts have continuously done so, all this century, in low orbit over Earth, on spaceships such as the International Space Shuttle (ISS). Thanks to their hard work and sacrifice, we've learned a lot—about what it's like to live in space and what we need to take up there with us.

The surface of the red planet is barren and inhospitable to human life—for now.

For decades, astronauts' escape suits have been bright orange for visibility in an emergency.

Do Astronauts Get Taller?

An era of human spaceflight ended on July 21, 2011, when the final space shuttle mission (STS-135, *Atlantis*) and its crew—Capt. Christopher Ferguson, Col. Douglas Hurley, Col. Rex Walheim, and Sandra Hall Magnus—landed at Kennedy Space Center in Florida.

As *Atlantis* touched down, its crew had collectively logged 11 spaceflights and more than 262 days in space. All that combined astronautic experience, though, would still be about one-fourth of that experienced by each human on a mission to Mars.

What happened to their bodies while they were up there? For one thing, they grew a total of about eight inches taller!

▶ **STRETCHING UP** Since gravity isn't tugging downward on their bones, astronauts in space can gradually grow up to 3 percent taller—nearly two inches for your typical spacefarer. Blood also flows more readily out of their feet and up into their heads, giving astronauts that puffy-cheeks look in zero gravity.

▶ **THE DOWNSIDE OF GETTING TALLER** That new-found height comes with a price, though. An astronaut in zero g can lose bone density up to 10 times faster than a 90-year-old person suffering from osteoporosis on Earth. After months of space travel, brittle bones can break from even a minor fall. Muscle strength can drop drastically, too. ∎

"You squish down pretty quickly, as soon as gravity hits you. You stand up—whoosh. Gravity is a pretty pervasive force."

—DR. SANDRA HALL MAGNUS, MISSION SPECIALIST, STS-135

Packing for Mars [Part 1]

Who'd Be the Ideal Candidates for Mars?

DID YOU KNOW

Astronaut and musician Chris Hadfield released an album he recorded on the ISS. *Space Sessions: Songs From a Tin Can* hit number 10 on Canadian charts in 2015.

Every person on a space mission is precious cargo, and the broader the set of skills and interests the crew spans, the more likely the mission will succeed.

Should we send artists and poets into space? We already do! They just also happen to be highly trained scientists, engineers, pilots, and technicians, plus great writers and speakers—even if most are quite modest about it. And someday in the not-so-distant future, space dreamers like musician Josh Groban will be packing for off-world travel, too.

What characteristics make the best astronaut—someone who will have to live with the same few people in tiny spaces for very long periods of time? Says Mary Roach, author of *Packing for Mars,* channeling certain cultural stereotypes: "The Japanese are, speaking very generally, good astronauts for a number of reasons: small payload, used to tiny spaces, not much privacy, and also, again, obviously speaking in generalities here, raised to be not confrontational and aggressive but polite and respectful." ■

Japanese astronaut Kimiya Yui

*"When I was a kid, my favorite costume was a space suit.
All day long, every day, I'd wear a space suit. And I was not Josh Groban
from Earth . . . I would say, 'I'm John from another planet.' "*

—JOSH GROBAN, MUSICIAN

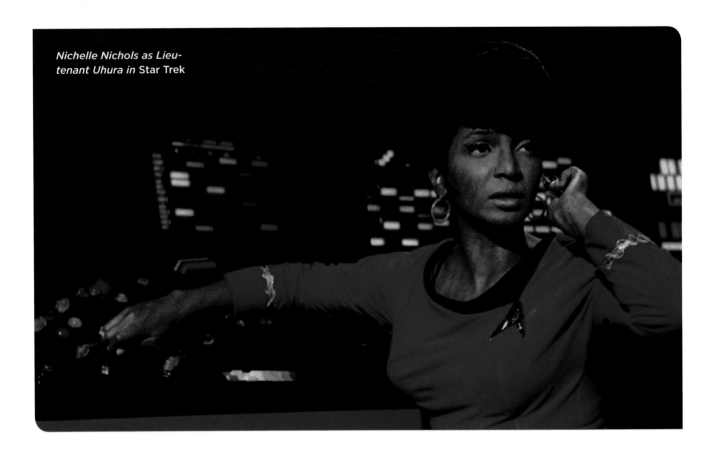

Nichelle Nichols as Lieutenant Uhura in Star Trek

NASA and Nichelle Nichols

How Did Nichelle Nichols Change the Face of NASA?

The starship Enterprise

Nichelle Nichols broke the television color barrier as *Star Trek*'s Lieutenant Uhura, the African-American communications officer on the starship *Enterprise*. When Nichols was asked by NASA to be part of the publicity campaign to recruit astronauts, her insistence that the astronaut corps include members of all races and genders helped create the diversity of humans in space today. As she puts it: "I said, 'I will help you, but I'm going to get you the most qualified people of anybody you've ever had, and therefore I don't want to hear any excuses, because they're going to apply in droves . . . and if there's not one woman and one person of color . . . I'll be your worst nightmare.'"

Little-known fact: Uhura's first name was never revealed in the *Star Trek* TV series. In the 2009 franchise-rebooting *Star Trek* movie, Spock appears to call her Nyota, but when Kirk tries to make it official, Spock says: "I have no comment on the matter . . ." ■

A space suit from Project Mercury

A suit worn on an Apollo mission

An ISS extravehicular mobility suit

StarTalk Live! From SF Sketchfest 2015

What Should I Wear to Go Exploring the Solar System?

> "Stay here on Earth. You can live the longest on Earth."
> —DR. NEIL DEGRASSE TYSON

But, hey, if you're going to disregard Neil's advice and explore the solar system, you need to stay alive and well—and you want to look good doing it. NASA's Solar System Exploration Research Virtual Institute (SSERVI)—dedicated to exploring Earth's moon, near-Earth asteroids, and Mars's two moons—can help.

Each of these destinations will have its own challenges. Most asteroids, for example, have so little gravitational pull that you can launch off the surface into space with just a running start. So your space suit will need a way to keep you connected to the ground! You'll also be vulnerable to plasma discharges, so your space suit will need enough metal to shield you from asteroidal lightning. ■

A space-suit glove allows for mobility.

Are We Floating in a Tin Can?

Scientists and engineers have been imagining and designing space stations—real ones, not crazy fictional Ringworlds and Death Stars—for more than a century. Working models, however, have only been around for about half that time.

‖‖‖‖‖
◀ SKYLAB 1973

The United States' first space station was almost destroyed during its launch, but the crew saved it in the world's first major in-space repair. Three human crews in all visited the 86-foot-long station, but delays to the space shuttle program doomed Skylab to fall back to Earth in 1979.

‖‖‖‖‖‖
▶ SALYUT 1 1971

The first space station occupied by humans launched on April 19, 1971. The three Soviet cosmonauts orbited for 23 days, but, tragically, suffocated on the return to Earth when their ship sprang a leak. Salyut 1 was de-orbited six months after its launch.

▶ MIR 1986

The U.S.S.R. launched a station similar in size to Skylab in 1986. The station—aptly named Mir, or "Peace"—survived the fall of the Soviet Union. Mir hosted 125 humans during 15 years of operation before being de-orbited on March 23, 2001.

||||||||
◀ TIANGONG 1 2011

The first Chinese-made space station held two crews of human visitors for several days in 2012 and 2013. It was the first of a series of stations, expected to culminate in a large ISS-like modular space station that will be launched in the 2020s.

||||||||
▶ INTERNATIONAL SPACE STATION (ISS) 1998

The ISS emerged from growing world cooperation and shrinking space budgets. Five space agencies jointly run the station, which has been continuously inhabited since November 2000 by spacefarers—including the world's first space tourists.

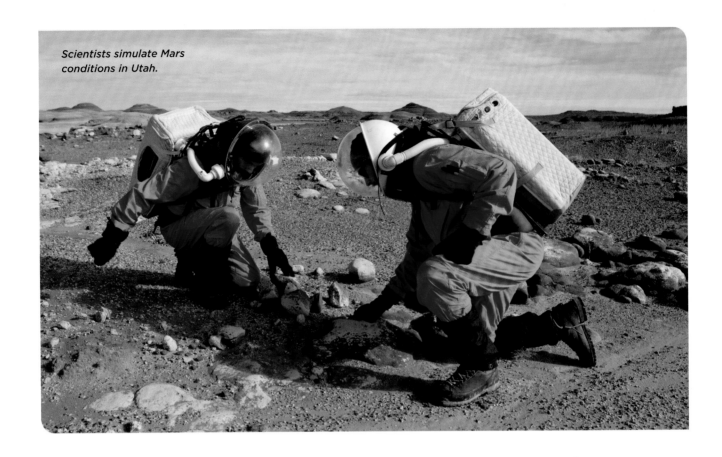

Scientists simulate Mars conditions in Utah.

What Can Antarctica Teach Us About Mars?

An Antarctic expedition reflected in a monument at the South Pole

You get to Mars and what you see is a vast, inhospitable frozen desert. So, coincidentally, is Antarctica. With its five million square miles of brutal isolation, it's the perfect place to study the effects of extended space missions on human health and psychology.

At Concordia, a European science station based in Antarctica, about a dozen intrepid people spend months at a time together in perpetual darkness, farther from civilization than the International Space Station is from Earth.

What happens to a person in that sort of situation? Here's what Mary Roach, author of *Packing for Mars,* says: "After about six weeks, you get this irrational antagonism that sets in, where the very things you loved about your crewmate initially begin to just drive you crazy."

It's not only your mood or your attitude; it's your body. Your immune system weakens. Your hormone levels go crazy. You can't sleep; you can't eat—it's like having perpetual jet lag. Figuring out ways to overcome these challenges will be essential to a successful Mars mission. ∎

Packing for Mars [Part 2]

Neil's Tips on Martian Sightseeing

Every day, humans are striving to get to Mars. If it happens, take advice from Neil and be sure to see everything the planet has to offer.

"I think of Mars as the American Southwest. There are beautiful structures that look great in the setting sun. There are different terrains that attract different kinds of interest. Mars is not just one destination . . . I would go to all of these places on different trips:

Mars has the largest volcano in the solar system, Olympus Mons.

If you're into valleys and riverbeds, you'd go to Valles Marineris, or Mariner Valley.

You can go to floodplains, places where water once flowed. And you have river deltas.

You can go to lakebeds that have long ago evaporated, leaving salty residue at the bottom—what we call precipitate if you want to be technical about it. It's no different than the Salt Lake in Utah. It used to be a liquid lake, the water evaporated leaving the salt behind.

I would not only look down, I would look up, and I would take a picture of Earth in the Martian sky.

Mars actually has two moons of its own: Phobos and Demos. They're kind of lame moons, one of them is like eight miles across—they're tiny. These are like Idaho potato–shaped, and near small.

And Mars has cool dust storms, too!" ■

The Olympus Mons shield volcano is 13.6 miles in height.

The 2,500-mile-long Valles Marineris runs along the Martian equator.

The floodplains span more than 960,000 square miles of the red planet.

What Would It Take to Get Neil to Go to Mars?

A s the possibility of moving to Mars comes closer to reality, some people are jumping at the chance and others are saying, "No way." What about Neil? He would take on the challenge as long as it could be a family adventure.

"If I could bring my family, and get a good [online media subscription service unnamed!] account and some books," Neil, the astro-settler-ist, proposes. "My wife is very well educated. We could both totally space-school—homeschool, spaceship-school—our kids, so then it's a family trip. I could totally do that."

Like all early pioneers who move beyond the

"Please, teach us again how great Earth was."
—JOHN OLIVER, ACTOR AND COMEDIAN

frontier into the new and unknown, Neil would pull up his earthly stakes, pack everyone into the Martian covered wagon, and blast off together. But comedian Eugene Mirman has a good point: "Yeah, but then your kids would be furious!"

Ah, not everyone sees migration to Mars as such a *Little House on the Prairie* utopian fantasy. The romanticization of the pioneer experience—immigration from Europe to the Americas, for example, or the settling of the western United States—glosses over the hardships, heartaches, and extreme danger along the way and after arrival, especially for children. ■

Neil discusses a future colony on Mars in Cosmos*—could he be a part of it?*

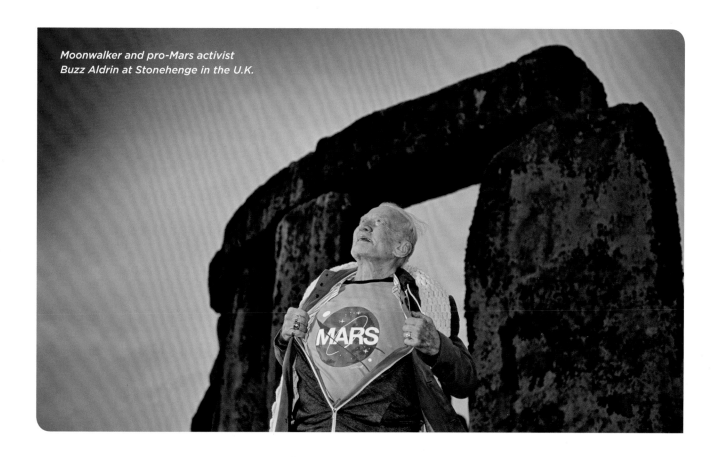

Moonwalker and pro-Mars activist
Buzz Aldrin at Stonehenge in the U.K.

How Would Buzz Aldrin Colonize Mars?

Water-ice clouds
hover in the Martian
atmosphere.

D r. Buzz Aldrin has written extensively—both fiction and nonfiction—about space travel, exploration, and colonization, including the book *Mission to Mars* (2013). He has proposed a plan, using a system of spacecraft continuously moving back and forth on orbits around Earth and Mars, to get people and necessities to Mars and establish a colony in a 20- to 30-year time frame. First, he believes a base on Phobos (the larger of Mars's two moons) should be built robotically. With enough commitment of resources, he argues, these plans are all technically feasible.

Maybe more important, *why* does Buzz want us to colonize Mars? For the same reason he went to the moon in 1969. It will be another giant leap for mankind. ■

"They will be the most remembered, the most talked about [people] that have ever set foot on Earth. Because they pioneered something that nobody ever did, and they carried it out."
—DR. BUZZ ALDRIN, ASTRONAUT

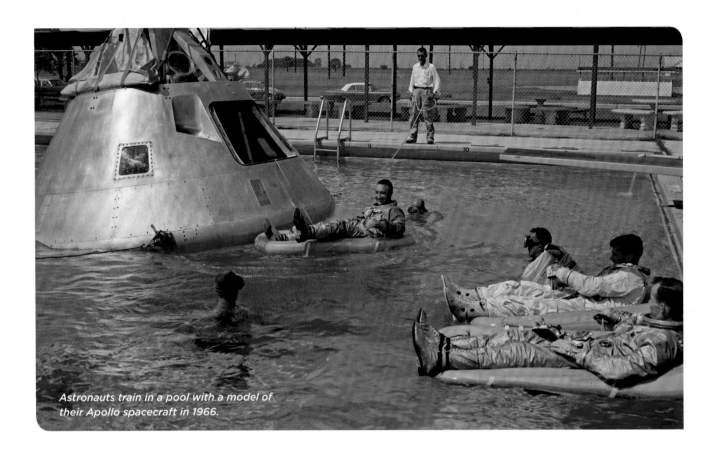

Astronauts train in a pool with a model of their Apollo spacecraft in 1966.

Why Did You Become an Astronaut?

"There is something about doing something borderline insane that does actually inspire people. Going to the moon was crazy—that was what was so incredible about it. Going around Mars barely makes any sense—so it's inherently inspirational . . . That's what America is built on. It's built on doing something that makes almost no sense to anyone else at the time."

—JOHN OLIVER,
ACTOR AND COMEDIAN

Neil Armstrong and Buzz Aldrin were military pilots before becoming astronauts. Col. Chris Hadfield and Dr. Mike Massimino, two later-generation astronauts, took different paths.

Col. Hadfield decided to become an astronaut when he was a boy: "I looked to my heroes Neil and Buzz and Mike Collins . . . Astronauts fly, so I learned to fly. The odds of being an astronaut are so tiny, that I wanted to do something that would lead to other things that sounded interesting to me anyway."

"I dreamt about being an astronaut . . . watching Neil Armstrong and Buzz Aldrin walk on the Moon," says Dr. Massimino. "Once I got out of college, I decided that's what I wanted to try to do. Went to graduate school, got my Ph.D., and started applying while . . . in grad school."

Astronauts all go through years of physical and psychological training. But the desire to go out into space, and the way to get to that threshold is what makes the corps of spacefarers diverse, capable, and strong. ∎

The International Space Station: A Space Age Cathedral

What's It Like on the International Space Station?

"When you first get into space, it feels a bit odd. It is a very unusual situation to be in. But depending on the person, your inner ear settles down very quickly. Mine settled down right away, and I had very little trouble adjusting to zero g."

Astronaut Dr. Shannon Walker shares her experience while aboard the ISS, Expedition 25: "There are so many things you can do when there's no gravity around. Of course, a lot of the fun things to do are things like playing with your food and making little bubbles and having them go here and there . . . Of course, we have to clean everything up, so we have to temper our excitement with the realities of keeping the station clean.

"I do look out the window a lot, whenever we have a chance to. The ground team keeps us pretty busy, and so we don't get to spend many hours looking out the window." ∎

TOUR GUIDE

How Do You Use the Bathroom in Space?

In space, even the mundane is an adventure. During the Apollo era, astronauts relieved themselves into plastic bags cupped over their crotches or taped to their buttocks. Now, there is a suction-based toilet that pulls the waste away. On the ISS, the liquid waste is purified into drinking water; solid waste is stored in containers until there's enough to launch it out of the station to burn up in Earth's atmosphere. (Maybe that shooting star you saw last night was actually a fiery fecal payload!)

Astronauts in zero g aboard the ISS

"Your angle of approach on a space toilet is important . . . It's a docking maneuver."

—MARY ROACH,
AUTHOR OF *PACKING FOR MARS*

"A total round-trip Mars mission is going to last three or four years, so what you really want is gardens on Mars. Create a hab module, and you can grow pigs and cows if you're carnivorous, or celery and carrots if you're veggie, and, you know, go to town."

—DR. NEIL DEGRASSE TYSON, ASTRO-FARMER-CIST

CHAPTER TWO

What Do I Eat in Space?

Human beings evolved on Earth over millions of years, from the rise of our first hominid ancestors to the present day. So did all of our food—and all of the living things that eat our food, and are thus eaten by us by accident. Indeed, every astronaut is a spaceship—home to trillions of microscopic life-forms, all eating and drinking and reproducing. Our digestive systems count on working in a terrestrial environment, so what happens when we bring them with us into outer space?

There are a lot of factors we'll have to take into account, big and small. What do you think, for example, happens when you drink carbonated soda in space, with no gravity in your stomach to separate the gas from the liquid? (Here's a hint: Burps in space aren't very dry.)

So, space gourmands, put aside that pressure cooker and put on your pressure suit. From appetizer to dessert, we're about to find out the best menu for our out-of-this-world journeys.

Feeding astronauts in space has required a lot of culinary creativity—but no food art yet.

Cosmic Cuisine

Why Can't I Get a Pulled Pork Sandwich in Space?

Astronauts can request their favorite menu items, but NASA has to test them. Capt. Sonny Carter, for instance, wanted pulled pork from Georgia, but it failed the test. Of course, Neil was concerned: "I thought nothing survives barbecuing . . . Did you alert him to how many microorganisms he was eating in his pulled pork?" As NASA food scientist Charles Bourland remembers: "Well, he didn't seem to be concerned about them. He'd been eating it all of his life."

Space food has to be squeaky-clean. Even if they're fully cooked, many well-known foods, especially meats, contain living microorganisms that are harmless on Earth but unwelcome—even dangerous—in spacecraft environments.

But meat has made it into space anyway. In 1965, astronaut John Young snuck a corned beef sandwich onto Gemini 3. By 1989, freeze-dried barbecued pork was on the space shuttle menu.

The best space food is wet—it needs to stick to the plate and fork. "If it's wet, surface tension will keep it on the utensil, so you can eat most things [in space . . . But] it has to be wet," explains Dr. Bourland. "If you open a packet of peanuts, it's all going to float away." ■

> It's not always the smartest person who makes a good astronaut. It's personality. You need to be able to live with someone for a long time—be unflappable and easy to get along with because you're confined in a small space for years.

Barbecue fans may find it hard to settle for freeze-dried meat in space.

MARY ROACH:
I tasted seven-year-life-span hash browns.

NEIL:
How were they?

MARY ROACH:
Eh.

THINK ON THIS ▶ Did You Remember to Bring Hot Sauce?

In dry environments with low atmospheric pressure—like space stations—human taste buds and noses don't work that well, so food tastes and smells bland. Chef and TV host Anthony Bourdain knows this well: "Apparently, if you have a stash of hot sauce, you're the go-to guy in outer space. They crave spice." Just be sure your spicy stuff is bacteria-free. A lot of hot sauces are fermented and thus full of microbes—generally a no-no in space.

DID YOU KNOW
South Korean food scientists spent years of research and millions of dollars to develop space-friendly kimchi—spicy fermented cabbage—for astronaut Ko San to bring aboard the ISS.

`Cosmic Queries: Space Tourism`

Who Wants a Ride on the Vomit Comet?

Enjoy your food in space, but good luck keeping it down. Just ask Neil: "I went into a centrifuge and I barfed up my lunch." What does astronaut Dr. Mike Massimino, expert at keeping his meals down, think of that? "I've never thrown up in a centrifuge. That's pretty sissy . . . I'm talking about in a spaceship."

Zero gravity confuses our digestive systems. Just think about how you feel during those brief near-free-fall moments on a roller coaster—and those puddles often found near the exit gate.

To train for space, NASA previously used a modified turbojet, the KC-135. It created a zero-g environment for 20 to 30 seconds at a time, and a typical mission hit zero g 30 or 40 times. Between 1995 and 2004, NASA cleaned at least 285 gallons of throw-up out of KC-135. The crew nicknamed the jet the Vomit Comet. ■

NASA's C-9 aircraft ascends at a sharp angle.

TOUR GUIDE

Neil's Tips on How to Avoid Motion Sickness in Space

"We live in one g. If that one g changes to any other kind of g, your body reacts. Your ear canals respond, your brain has to try to reconcile what's going on, and in the effort to do so, you get an upset stomach. Motion sickness, it's called. However, once you're in zero g, you can get accustomed to that, because the g-force isn't changing. The first sign of motion sickness is sleepiness. So if the motion sickness is mild, you'll just go to sleep. That means that in space, if you're going from one location to another, see if you can park yourself at that first symptom and just sleep through it."

"With the Vomit Comet . . . they make sure you don't eat for 6, 8, 12 hours before, so now your stomach has got nothing in it to give. So they've reduced—sort of— the vomiting factor, and you just have fun."
—DR. NEIL DEGRASSE TYSON, ASTRO-PUKE-ICIST

What's for Dinner?

Astronaut food has evolved from necessary nutrients to real cuisine. You may not recognize their names, though. According to astronaut Dr. Mike Massimino, NASA doesn't like to advertise brands: "We have a certain candy that's very popular because they're small and you can float them, and we call them 'candy-coated chocolates.'"

1962

◀ Astronaut John Glenn, the first American to eat in space, had applesauce, pureed beef, and vegetables in aluminum tubes on Friendship 7.

1969

◀ This small stainless steel spoon was used by command module pilot Michael Collins during the Apollo 11 mission. It was part of his personal preference kit.

1973

▶ The Skylab program introduced refrigerated food and a galley kitchen to space. Astronauts finally got to have ice cream!

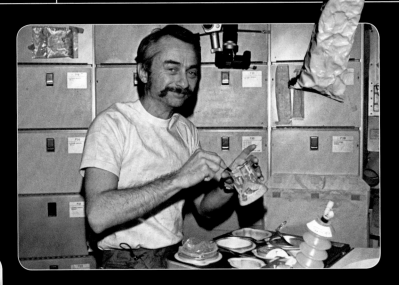

1992

▲ A popular choice for astronauts was M&M's, officially known as "candy-coated chocolates" on spacecraft.

2007

◀ TV chef Martha Stewart designed a gourmet freeze-dried meal for her boyfriend traveling to the ISS as a space tourist. The meals were prepared by French chef Alain Ducasse's ADF consulting center.

1965

▶ Project Gemini introduced the first freeze-dried food—a beef sandwich, strawberry cereal cubes, peaches, and beef gravy. At the same time, an astronaut smuggled a deli sandwich into space, but he couldn't eat it because it started to disintegrate.

1968

▼ Astronauts celebrated Christmas Day in space with thermostabilized turkey with gravy and cranberry sauce.

1975

◀ On a joint mission, Russian astronauts shared tubes of borscht (beet soup).

2015

◀ Astronauts made history on the ISS in 2015 when they grew the first successful food in space—romaine lettuce!

FOOD FOR THOUGHT

Did NASA Invent Tang?

Short answer: no. "Tang was on the grocery shelf before NASA was even formed," says Dr. Charles Bourland, a NASA food scientist. Tang was created in 1957 and hit stores in 1959. It first went into space in 1962 with John Glenn—and a culinary myth was born.

The famous drink mix—just add water!—was assembled by the food chemist Bill Mitchell, who earned dozens of patents in his illustrious career. Mitchell was the creator of many an edible invention, including artificial tapioca pudding, powdered egg whites, Pop Rocks, instant-set Jell-O gelatin, and Cool Whip. ▪

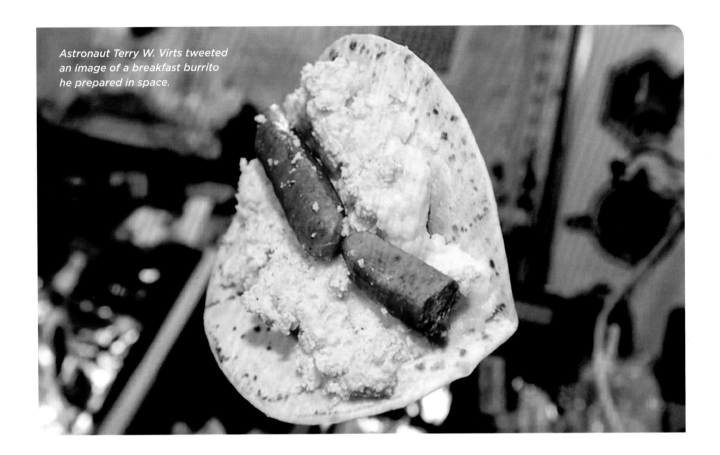

Astronaut Terry W. Virts tweeted an image of a breakfast burrito he prepared in space.

Cosmic Queries: Human Endurance in Space

Can I Get That on a Tortilla?

All ISS astronauts have a small amount of payload space they can fill with foods of their choice to eat while in orbit. Within the limits of space-approved munchies, the variety is vast—like, for example, astronaut Chris Hadfield's peanut-butter-and-honey tortilla wraps! "All astronauts take comfort food with them," Neil says. "There's meat loaf, there's rice and beans, there's tortillas. Tortillas are great because they don't make crumbs when you eat them." ■

▶ HOW QUICKLY WOULD A PIZZA BAKE ON VENUS?

"A 16-inch pizza would cook in nine seconds on the windowsill." —Neil

9 secs

▶ HOW QUICKLY WOULD COFFEE FREEZE IN SPACE?

With an airtight lid, a radiatively cooling cup o' joe would take several hours to freeze solid.

2+ hours

Packing for Mars (Part 1)

How 'bout I Just Have Some Lasagna?

Of course, astronauts are tough enough that they'd be willing to eat anything they need to survive, but the point of space food is to make the space travelers happy as well as healthy. You would think ice cream would do it, but as food scientist Dr. Charles Bourland explains: "An interesting story about astronaut ice cream is that it was only used on Apollo 8 . . . and they denied eating any of it . . . I don't know if they were too chicken, or if they didn't like it, but later on when we tested it with other astronauts, they didn't like it because it sticks to your teeth."

The kitchen on Skylab, NASA's space station of the 1970s, actually had a refrigerator. There isn't one on the ISS, but the astronauts there still have more than 200 menu items to choose from. "The food actually is pretty good in space, and it's easy to cook. You just add water, you put it in the oven," says astronaut Dr. Mike Massimino. "My favorite was the lasagna. Not quite [like Mama made it] but it was easy to cook [and] it was delicious. We had lasagna, ravioli . . . that's my comfort food. On Sundays I'd have my lasagna, and every other day of the week, [too]." ■

NEIL TWEETS

Cosmic Eats

"Here's what you do, next Mars mission, bring all the food that has space names to it. No food named Uranus . . . Here we go:"

Eclipse mints

Milky Way bar

Moon Pie

Sunkist

THINK ON THIS ▶ How Do You Make Astronaut Ice Cream?

"Freeze-drying. If I remember my food science, you blow air across the food while it's frozen, and then you evaporate or sublimate the frozen water, leaving behind the flavor and everything else that is the ice cream."
—Dr. Neil deGrasse Tyson, astro-cream-icist

Blue cheese gets its flavor and color from the penicillin fungus

Do You Want Microbes With That?

Pickled vegetables can be good for our gut health.

Decomposition is a totally natural thing on Earth, even when it happens in your refrigerator. Neil explains why: "Why does food decompose? Because there are microbes in it, eating it before you have a chance to get there." And germophobia aside, a little rotting isn't necessarily bad. Indeed, some of the most expensive steaks are dry-aged at room temperature for up to three weeks as they crust over with mold. Before cooking, the surface is cut away, revealing the extra-tender, extra-flavorful pink stuff underneath.

And then there are pickles, sauerkraut, miso, cheese . . . And nutritionists say fermented foods are good for us. ■

"I visited the NASA 'cosmic kitchen' at Johnson Space Center in Houston . . . I had a steak that had been in a packet on the shelf for five years, unrefrigerated. Some foods they just have to irradiate."

—DR. NEIL DEGRASSE TYSON, ASTRO-NAUT-FOOD-IST

Packing for Mars [Part 1]

Houston, We've Got a Food Problem

In the early days of spaceflight, NASA astronauts were fed dried cubes of solid food or squeeze tubes of liquid food. The food scientists behind space cuisine at the time weren't concerned with the flavor of the food. Their focus was on nutrition—making sure astronauts got the vitamins, protein, and minerals needed on their missions. As a result, the menu wasn't tasty, and the food delivery systems didn't do a very good job. (Imagine pureeing a hamburger into the consistency of baby food and squeezing it into your mouth like toothpaste.) Astronauts, not surprisingly, complained bitterly—including astronaut Jim Lovell, who directly insulted the meal-creating ability of NASA food scientists while on board Gemini 7. He sent a scathing review of NASA's chicken à la king (see above) back home via NASA's official memo system.

Things got better toward the end of the Gemini era. The squeeze tubes were replaced by plastic pouches of freeze-dried food that could be easily rehydrated. Bite-size cubes came in a plastic container that made reconstituting easier. The new packaging made menu options better, too. Later Gemini astronauts enjoyed choices such as shrimp cocktail, chicken and vegetables, and butterscotch pudding.

By the Apollo era, spoons and forks had become the norm, as did hot water to make rehydrating foods easier. Skylab brought the next big boost in space food. With room for a dining room table, astronauts could choose from an extensive menu featuring 72 different food items. ∎

"[On] Gemini 7, Jim Lovell was taking it out on the nutritionist, the guy who invented the food [in the mission transcripts]. 'Memo to Dr. Chance: Chicken à la King Serial Number 654. Cannot even squeeze food through neck.'"

—MARY ROACH, AUTHOR OF *PACKING FOR MARS*

Grilled pork chops aren't on the menu.

DID YOU KNOW

Food for the Mercury and Gemini missions was designed in part to reduce the need for the astronauts to use the bathroom—after all, there *weren't* any bathrooms on those spacecraft.

THINK ON THIS ▶ Why Not Just Send Plump People to Space?

"The most extreme approach that I saw was this guy who suggested, and I think he was being serious, that NASA should recruit obese astronauts. He figured out that for 50 pounds of excess weight there's like 184,000 calories. You would just basically starve the astronaut for the duration of the mission." —Mary Roach, author of *Packing for Mars*

"If you take the three-dimensionality of our universe and then you embed it among other universes in another kind of space, that's a higher dimension . . . You step out of your dimension, and then the walls no longer contain you."

—DR. NEIL DEGRASSE TYSON, ASTROPHYSICIST

CHAPTER THREE

Can We Use Wormholes to Travel?

Humans can get to the Moon and back in about three days. To Mars and back, we'd take about three years. To the nearest star system other than ours, though—Alpha Centauri, about 4.4 light-years away—it would take more than 300 *centuries* just to get there. Obviously, we don't have that much time. So what in the universe might we use to cut our travel time?

When we ask that kind of question, what we're really asking is this: What *don't* we know about the universe today that will lead us to tomorrow's physics, paradigms, and, ultimately, technology? Might it be so-called dark matter and dark energy, which together make up 95 percent of the universe's contents? Or might it be black holes?

Let's start with the idea of wormholes—shortcut tunnels through warped space and time. The idea of wormholes has been around for a long time, but always as science fiction. However, confirmation within the past half century of black holes as real cosmic objects has led to brainwork connecting fiction with reality.

Will we one day be able to cross dimensions via a wormhole?

Is a Wormhole Bigger on the Inside?

> *"The question is, 'Is there any form of energy in the universe that's capable of keeping the wormhole sort of afloat?'"*
> —DR. JANNA LEVIN, COSMOLOGIST

A wormhole is essentially some kind of warp, channel, or bubble that cuts in and through space-time. Wormholes are pervasive in science fiction, because they represent a way to travel vast distances instantaneously—if they can be controlled.

Fact is, scientists today really think there might be such things. The mathematics of wormholes is highly speculative, but we're learning more about them all the time. "Wormholes, although they are probably theoretically possible, are physically, as far as we know, still impossible," says astrophysicist and author Dr. Janna Levin. "[A wormhole] can be a lot bigger on the inside than it is on the outside . . . To keep the throat open of the wormhole, you need forms of matter and energy that we've never seen before. We don't know anything that could actually keep the throat open on a wormhole. They will keep closing up. It's very unstable."

So the biggest limitation is not the mathematical possibilities, but the energy requirements to control a wormhole. Ten trillion trillion trillion watts of power—the combined output of every star in our galaxy put together—might do it. We're not sure, and it's hard to figure it out in a science lab. ∎

A conceptual computer rendering of a wormhole through space

DID YOU KNOW

The TARDIS of *Doctor Who* fame isn't just a machine that harnesses wormhole technology—it has sentience and intelligence, too.

THINK ON THIS ▶ Could We Control Wormholes Like in the Movies?

"One of my favorite scenes in *Monsters, Inc.*, undiscussed in the reviews of the movie, is that . . . that movie was all about wormholes. Those doors were wormholes . . . wormholes connecting the factory to everybody's closet." —Dr. Neil deGrasse Tyson, astro-worm-icist

Live at the Bell House (Part 1)

Spaghetti? Me? (Or Neil's Death by Black Hole)

If you're going to visit space, it's best to avoid black holes at all costs. "But what if something awesome is on the other side?" asks Kristen Schaal, actress and comedian.

OK, Kristen, get ready. Here's what will happen when you get too close to a black hole:

▶ STEP ONE

As you fall toward the black hole, the gravity that you experience begins to grow. The gravity at your feet starts becoming greater than the gravity at your head by ever increasing margins. In other words, you're going to get taller.

▶ STEP TWO

The force will eventually exceed the intermolecular bonds that keep your flesh together in one human form. Your body bifurcates, snapping into two pieces, probably separating at your lower spine.

▶ STEP THREE

Meanwhile this tidal force continues, and the two halves of you will continue to stretch. And so your upper half will split into two, as will your lower half. You are now 4 pieces in a train going down, which continues to split, 4, 8, 16, 32 . . . so at one point you will be 210 pieces as you continue to bifurcate.

Comedian Kristen Schaal

▶ STEP FOUR

As you come down to the point that is the center of the black hole, your body funnels down into a narrower and narrower zone. Your pieces will come together left to right, but not top to bottom. So you have been extruded through the fabric of space like toothpaste through a tube. ∎

NEIL TWEETS

One Way to Die . . . by Falling Into a Black Hole

In a feet-first dive
To this cosmic abyss,
You will not survive
Because you will not miss.
The tidal forces of gravity
Will create quite a calamity,
When you're stretched head to toe—
Are you sure you want to go?
Your body's atoms—you'll see them!
Will enter one by one;
The singularity will eat 'em—
And you won't be having fun.

—A POEM BY DR. NEIL DEGRASSE TYSON

DID YOU KNOW

Supermassive black holes would tear you apart less violently than small black holes as you fall into them. The tidal forces—the difference in the strength of gravity between two points—are not as extreme.

Cosmic Queries: New Discoveries

Could a Black Hole Be Destroyed?

DID YOU KNOW
The largest black hole that could have evaporated since the big bang would have to have been smaller than an atomic nucleus.

Physicist Stephen Hawking first came up with the mathematical formulation showing that, thanks to quantum mechanical processes just inside its event horizon, a black hole can lose mass and shrink over time. How long would it take? A verrrrry loooong time, says Neil: "We call it 'Hawking radiation.' The stuff that goes into a black hole slowly evaporates out of the black hole, until the black hole one day disappears entirely. It's very slow. Takes 10^{100} years to evaporate a super-massive black hole. A goo-gol years."

"Black holes are stronger than any nuclear fusion . . . That's why we got the black hole in the first place. The black hole used to be a star. The star was going to explode, and it didn't. The black hole said, 'No, you're not!' "

—DR. NEIL DEGRASSE TYSON, ASTRO-FUSE-ICIST

Could anything else destroy a black hole? Black holes could crash into one another. In 2015 such an event, more than a billion light-years from Earth, was detected by the burst of gravitational wave radiation it emitted. The black holes weren't destroyed, though—they just merged to make an even bigger black hole. ∎

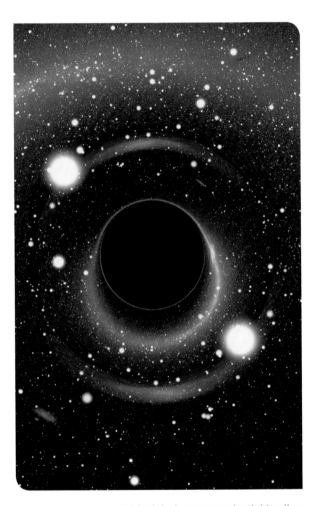

A black hole warps celestial bodies.

THINK ON THIS ▶ Could Nuclear Fusion Destroy a Black Hole?

Nuclear fusion, the power source of hydrogen bombs, is the most powerful force humans have ever harnessed. Massive stars, the birthplaces of black holes, can generate more energy with nuclear fusion in one-trillionth of a second than the explosive power of all the world's hydrogen bombs put together. And even that's not enough to do *anything* to a black hole.

Cosmic Queries With Bill Nye and Astro Mike

How Big Can a Star Get Before It Becomes a Black Hole?

Stars produce black holes when, late in their lives, their inward gravitational pull overwhelms their outward energy output. In stars, mass and size don't always correspond; the Sun, for example, will never make a black hole, but for part of its 10-billion-year lifetime it'll be bigger than a more massive star that would make one.

"So would you describe it as over a million whales?" asks comedian Eugene Mirman. Sure, we can use whales to try to get a handle on stars. The sun has a mass of 10 million million million million adult blue whales! That's big, but not big enough. If a star is less than 8 times the mass of the Sun, it's probably not going to make a black hole. If it's more than 20 times, it'll probably make one. In between, it could go either way. ■

BIOGRAPHY

Who Is Vera Rubin?

Vera Rubin (1928–2016) pushed the frontier of cosmic understanding from the very start of her career. Two decades before cosmic large-scale structure was confirmed, Rubin concluded in her 1954 doctoral dissertation that galaxies were clustered unevenly throughout the universe. Her work on the rotational motion of the outskirts of spiral galaxies proved that galaxies are embedded within huge halos of dark matter that far outweigh their stars. She was the first woman to make her own observations as an official guest investigator at Palomar Observatory in California, and the second woman ever to be elected to the National Academy of Sciences.

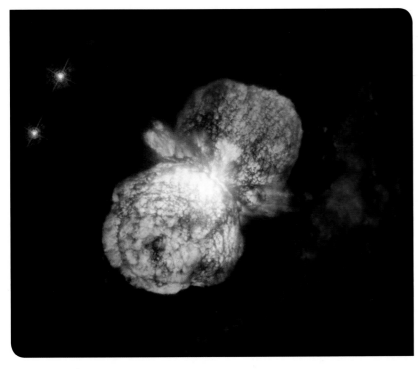

Hubble captures gas and dust billowing from a supermassive star.

"We see black holes in the center of every galaxy we've had the power to look into . . . and when you do, you can say, 'I bet you were a quasar back in your youth.'"

—DR. NEIL DEGRASSE TYSON

Exotic Matter in the Universe

What we call "exotic" matter isn't really that weird, cosmically speaking. We just don't encounter these forms of matter under normal circumstances here on Earth, in our narrow environmental ranges of temperature, pressure, and density. And for our well-being, that's probably a good thing! Out in the universe, though, this stuff is all over the place.

IIIIIII

◀ ELECTRON-DEGENERATE MATTER

In white dwarfs—remnants of stars about the mass of the Sun—gravity presses atoms so close together that a spoonful would weigh several tons. There's some of this material at the center of the Sun right now.

IIIIIII

▶ NEUTRON-DEGENERATE MATTER

In neutron stars—remnants of stars about 10 times the mass of the Sun—atoms have been destroyed by the intense gravity, and nuclear material is pressed tightly together. A spoonful would weigh several *billion* tons.

◀ BLACK HOLES

We have no way to tell what states matter takes within the event horizon of a black hole—nothing can get out from there in a form we can interpret. There's likely to be a singularity at the center that approaches zero volume and infinite density, but it's impossible to be sure.

▶ STRANGE MATTER

The protons and neutrons in ordinary atoms are made of two types of quarks, called up quarks and down quarks. At superhigh densities, perhaps at the centers of neutron stars, a third kind of quark—"strange"—could hypothetically combine with up and down quarks to create highly unstable versions of the subatomic particles we know.

◀ DARK MATTER

Strangelets, axions, weakly interacting massive particles (WIMPs), huge WIMP-like particles called "WIMPzillas" —none of these hypothetical particles have ever been observed, but they might fit the theoretical requirements of more than 80 percent of the mass in the universe.

"We explore the solar system and the rest of the cosmos with our robots, which are basically our eyes and our ears. So it's great: I get to go explore the cosmos from the comfort of my couch, which I love. I can still eat doughnuts . . . It's a much better life."

—DR. AMY MAINZER, ASTROPHYSICIST

CHAPTER FOUR

Who Goes There?

As humanity takes its first steps beyond its home planet, what are we sending (who), how are they traveling (goes), and where are they going (there)?

Right now, we're sending robotic spacecraft, filled with scientific sensors and communications equipment. What has their use taught us about space—and about ourselves? They're extensions of us, after all, our remote eyes and ears. If these robots also had brains, would they still be "us"—or would they become "them"?

Robots or humans, our intrepid explorers are looking for wonders yet unimagined. Maybe the most commonly imagined wonder, though, is extraterrestrial life! We think we're most likely to find simple life-forms—unicellular microbes, or algae, or primitive plants and animals. The chance is there, though, that we'll find intelligent creatures—who, upon seeing us snooping around the cosmos, might well indeed ask us: Who goes there?

NASA's robot Valkyrie is six feet tall and weighs 290 pounds.

Do Scientists Really Look Like Their Spacecraft?

Every space probe embodies the work of hundreds or even thousands of people and their collective blood, sweat, toil, and tears. So, like Dr. Frankenstein in Mary Shelley's classic novel, are these scientists and their visages revealed in the form of their creations?

||||||

◄ WIDE-FIELD INFRARED SURVEY EXPLORER (WISE), DR. AMY MAINZER

Launched in December 2009, WISE is a four-channel supercooled infrared telescope. The telescope's mission is to survey the entire sky, with 1,000 times more sensitivity than all previous infrared missions.

||||||

▶ LIGHTSAIL, BILL NYE

Built with reflective sails, LightSail completed a test flight in June 2015 and is expected to set sail again in 2017. The spacecraft—a citizen-funded project by the Planetary Society—uses the Sun's energy for propulsion—flight by light.

||||||||

◀ SPIRIT AND
OPPORTUNITY,
DR. STEVEN SQUYRES

As part of the Mars exploration
rover mission, Spirit traveled
4.8 miles on the surface of
Mars between 2004 and 2010.
Opportunity, its twin,
has traveled more than
25 miles since 2004.

||||||||

◀ CASSINI,
DR. CAROLYN PORCO

Launched in 1997, Cassini entered
Saturn's orbit in 2004. Its mission
includes studying the planet's rings,
atmosphere, and moons.

||||||||

▲ CURIOSITY,
DR. DAVID GRINSPOON

Curiosity landed near Mars's
Gale crater on August 6, 2012.
The rover was still operational
as of spring 2016.

"So, literally, aliens can come to Earth, say hello in 55 languages, and then murder people. Literally, 55 nations will let their guard down, maybe more."

—EUGENE MIRMAN, COMEDIAN

StarTalk Live!: I, Robot (Part 1)

What's So Special About Voyager 1?

In 2012 the Voyager 1 space probe entered interstellar space, 35 years after it took off from Earth. It was the first human creation to do so. Its instruments recorded a change in the environment around it, proving it had crossed the threshold of the Sun's electromagnetic influence. It now takes light and radio waves nearly 20 hours to get from Voyager 1 to Earth, and the spacecraft is now more than 12 billion miles from Earth.

"What's special about Voyager is that it was launched with enough energy to career around Jupiter and Saturn," Neil says. "By the time it exited the solar system it had enough speed to leave the solar system entirely, and upon doing so, just recently it actually crossed the border between our solar system and space. The farthest object we have ever sent anywhere, ever."

And it's still working great! NASA's plan is to continue using Voyager to obtain science data on interplanetary and interstellar fields, particles, and waves until at least 2020. All this with a machine whose available onboard computer memory is about .000002 gigabyte—one ten-millionth that of a typical smartphone. ∎

Voyager 1 launches aboard a Titan rocket in 1977.

TOUR GUIDE

What's on the Golden Record?

Low-tech by today's standards, a gold-plated vinyl record rides on both Voyager 1 and Voyager 2, along with nonverbal instructions on how to build a machine to play it. Each record carries:

▶ More than 100 images, including mathematical equations and information about our solar system and its location, the planets, human anatomy, plants, animals, an astronaut, the United Nations building, and a supermarket.

▶ A spoken greeting in English by the secretary-general of the United Nations.

▶ A wide variety of natural and human-made sounds, such as those of ocean surf, wind, thunder, crickets, frogs, birds, whales, and laughter.

▶ 90 minutes of musical selections by classical and jazz composers, and from numerous folk traditions.

▶ Spoken greetings from humans in 55 languages, including ancient Greek, Akkadian, and Sumerian.

▶ The Latin message *per aspera ad astra* ("through challenges, to the stars") in Morse code.

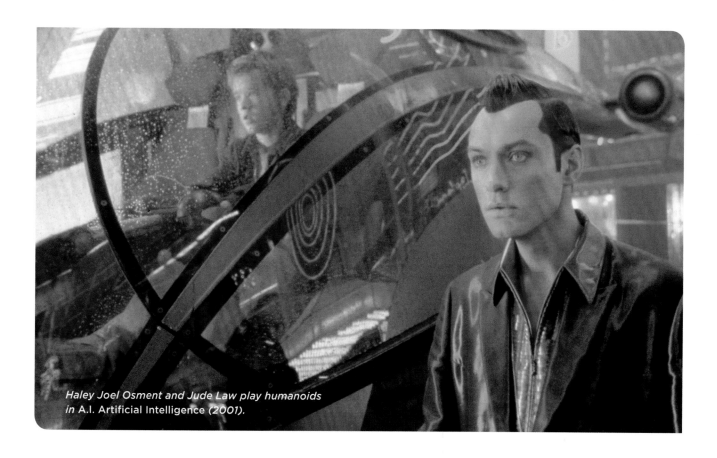

Haley Joel Osment and Jude Law play humanoids
in A.I. Artificial Intelligence (2001).

Are Robots "Them" or "Us"?

An industrious
Wall-E toy from
Disney-Pixar

The philosophical definition of what makes us human doesn't include distinctions between biological or mechanical bodies. We may make "them" mechanically, but we make copies of "us" biologically. So what if they're not as advanced as we are yet? Human reproduction took four billion years to evolve, and we've only been making robots for about four decades.

And what do we mean by "advanced," anyway? Without technology, humans aren't advanced enough to travel deep into interplanetary space, or roam the Martian surface without food, or analyze Saturn's magnetic field. But our robots can. ■

"We shouldn't dismiss these robots as saying that that's not like sending humans, because we are . . . We outsource our cognition to these robots. The mind of man crawls Mars at the moment."

—JASON SILVA, FUTURIST

What Is a Robot, Really?

Like so many words, the word "robot" means something in day-to-day conversation that is different from its technical usage. Creations we would certainly call robots today were imagined even in ancient times. The Greek god Hephaestus, it is said, built metal automatons to serve him. According to Greek mythology, by the way, Hephaestus also constructed Pandora, the first woman. In any case, robots—of either the hardware or software variety—need to have a certain level of complexity, flexibility, and in some cases even a capacity to learn. Even those terms, though, have varying definitions, depending on whom you ask.

> "If a person introduced the robot to me as a human, I would deal with it that way, because I don't know what this person's deal is. I don't want to judge."
> —JASON SUDEIKIS, COMEDIAN

Here's roboticist and space scientist Stephen Gorevan's definition: "A robot is a programmable manipulator. Now I realize that sounds more like a cross between a computer and my ex-wife, but if a machine doesn't do more than a few things, it's not really a robot . . . If it does sort of one thing or a short classification of things, then it's an automated spacecraft." ∎

> *"When it manipulates things, I think that's what makes it a robot."*
> —STEPHEN GOREVAN, ROBOTICIST AND SPACE SCIENTIST

LAUGH OUT LOUD ▶ **With "Mars Czar" Dr. G. Scott Hubbard**

"It's very difficult to compare the generic robotic mission with the generic human exploration mission, but sending humans, because of the life support and all the other issues, is at least 10 times, maybe as much as 100 times, more expensive . . . Assuming you want to keep them all alive."

Where's the Sense of Adventure?

We want to live vicariously through our adventure heroes, and imagine that we're making these exciting scientific discoveries and pioneering things ourselves. Is achieving these tasks by machine simply not as good as doing so in person?

Planetary scientist Steven Squyres may think so: "I have spent the last 20 years of my life trying to design and operate robots that can replicate what a human might be able to do on the Martian surface. What our rovers do in a day, you and I could do in about 30 seconds . . . Humans have a capability to synthesize information, to digest it, to figure out the next thing to do, and to improvise. Robots can't improvise the way humans can."

So, yes, sooner or later we really should send people to Mars or wherever we want to study. "Humans [also] have a capability to inspire that robots simply lack," says Squyres. "Someone once famously said, 'No one's ever going to give a robot a ticker-tape parade.'"

But until we can go safely, robots will pave the way. ∎

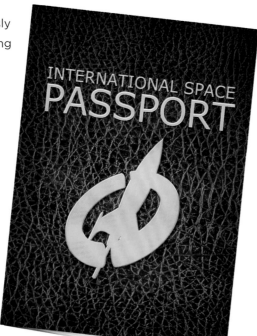

One day, we all may carry these passports as we travel through space.

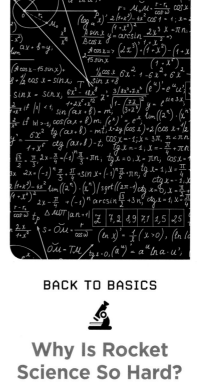

BACK TO BASICS

Why Is Rocket Science So Hard?

Rocket science deals with a lot of energy being released, a lot of force being applied, and a lot of mass being moved a long way. One seemingly small error can have huge consequences. Here are just three examples:

2003: The space shuttle *Columbia* burns up during reentry into Earth's atmosphere, killing all seven astronauts aboard. The leading edge of the left wing was damaged during launch, causing the orbiter's thermal protection system to fail.

2011: The Russian probe Phobos-Grunt, designed to bring rock samples back from a Martian moon, gets stuck in low-Earth orbit and crashes into the Pacific Ocean two months after launch. At least one rocket failed to fire properly.

2015: A SpaceX Falcon 9 rocket disintegrates in midair two minutes after launch. A single support strut failed, causing catastrophic structural failure of the entire rocket.

How Do Spacecraft Move in Space With Nothing to Push On?

A vintage tin rocket racer toy

One of the most common misconceptions about space travel is that in order to move, you have to push off something, like Earth's surface. "When you watch the rocket leave the ground, it gives you the impression that the flames and gases are pushing against the Earth, but that's not really what's going on," explains Bill Nye the Science Guy. "You're throwing hot gas out the back of the rocket so fast that the reaction is the rocket goes off in the other direction . . . This works whether you're on the Earth or in space."

Newton's third law of motion—for every action, there is an equal and opposite reaction—means that the simple act of pushing is enough; you don't need to push *on* or *off* any external object or surface to generate motion.

Some rockets and nonrocket systems, like the Hubble, use reaction wheels to move. "You spin them in a certain direction and you get a reaction in the other direction," says astronaut Dr. Mike Massimino. "Then the thing will point where you want it." ∎

> "We're going to have this very large sail deployed from this . . . tiny spacecraft . . . You steer it by tacking, the same way you steer a sailing ship."
> —BILL NYE, THE SCIENCE GUY, SPEAKING OF LIGHTSAIL, A SUNLIGHT-POWERED SPACECRAFT

> "People worried . . . suppose [it] enters our atmosphere and then disintegrates, then it scatters plutonium around the world, killing everyone. So there were some protests at the time . . . It didn't happen, because we know Newton's laws of motion. We got this one."
> —DR. NEIL DEGRASSE TYSON, ASTRO-NUKE-ICIST

THINK ON THIS ▸ Have We Been Sending Nukes Into Space?

Some nuclear reactors have been sent into orbit, but not yet on scientific space probes. Radioactive materials, on the other hand, have been used often; their radioactive decay produces the small amount of steady heat used by radioisotope thermoelectric generators (RTGs) to power the probes' electrical systems. The RTGs are heavily shielded and have never endangered humans on Earth.

Why Did Lowell Think There Was Life on Mars?

Percival Lowell (1855–1916) was the black sheep of a wealthy Boston family, the brother of poet Amy Lowell and Harvard president Abbott Lowell. He founded Lowell Observatory in northern Arizona—still a world-leading research institution today—and studied Mars from there for two decades.

Lowell is famous for announcing that he observed canals engineered on the surface of Mars. "People looked through a telescope a hundred years ago, and in moments of brief atmospheric clarity they could see what looked like a fine network of straight lines on the planet's surface," says planetary scientist Dr. Steven W. Squyres. "And they were so straight and so regular that the people looking at these concluded that not only were they evidence of life, but they were evidence of intelligent life. Now they were correct, but the life was at the wrong end of the telescope. What they were seeing was an optical illusion. In fact, there's nothing of the sort on the surface of Mars."

Lowell's mistake didn't make him any less of a scientist, though. His evidence was flawed, but his efforts were earnest, and mistakes are part of the process of discovery. Lowell would have been a bad scientist only if he had clung to his incorrect position against clear scientific evidence—which, at the time, was unavailable. ■

TOUR GUIDE

Will We Find Life Inside or Outside Our Solar System?

The exploding number of known exoplanets—planets outside our solar system, orbiting stars other than the Sun—has made some scientists think we'll have better luck looking beyond. There are, after all, thousands of exoplanets and only one Mars! That said, Neil still thinks we'll find life on Mars first: "On Mars, it's the microbial life we're eager to find . . . If we find life on exoplanets, we're not looking at it microbially . . . We're at the cusp of being able to look at the atmospheric chemistry of planets that are orbiting other stars . . . We'll find life sooner on Mars than on an exoplanet, just because the technology isn't completely there yet."

Could Life on Earth Have Originated on Mars?

Here's what we know so far according to Neil: "We learned only recently that when an asteroid hits, surrounding rocks can be thrust back into space and recoil with sufficient ferocity that they can escape the planet altogether . . . And, we have found, if you have a rock with nooks and crannies, and if the originating planetary surface is rich with life, and that rock escapes the planetary surface, it can have stowaway microbes that can survive the vacuum of interplanetary space. So the rock moves through space and lands on another planet. We have a word for this—it's called panspermia."

The tastefulness of the term aside, panspermia is only possible if the microbes survive a brutal interplanetary journey—and one that lasts millions, if not billions, of years. Experiments and computer simulations suggest a very, very low probability of such survival. On the other hand, the entire microbe may not have to survive—maybe its molecular constituents alone, like protein or RNA or DNA, would do the trick.

"So here's the thing," says Neil. "Evidence shows that Mars, as a planet, was wet and fertile earlier than Earth was. That being the likelihood, a rock from Mars could have been infused with microbes from there and, landing on Earth, it could have spawned life as we know it. Which would tell us then that all life on Earth descends from Martians." ■

The fiery crash landing of an asteroid on Earth

StarTalk Live!: **Exploring Our Funky Solar System**

What's Biting on Europa?

Jupiter's moon Europa, slightly smaller than Earth's moon, is covered with a thick layer of frozen water. Its surface is scarred with ridges, cracks, and seams, much like Earth's polar ice caps. Deep below this icy surface, could there be a vast underground liquid ocean? Could there be life? We're looking for it, according to astrobiologist Dr. David Grinspoon: "Europa is NASA's top priority for a big mission, because it's one of the places where there ought to be life, if we're right about what it takes for life. There's an ocean, we think, beneath this icy crust. In fact, it may be our solar system's biggest ocean of liquid water."

> *"I want to be the first person to eat a space lobster.* Deadliest Catch: Europa."
>
> —EUGENE MIRMAN, COMEDIAN

It's not a sure thing, of course; life exists in Earth's oceans under thick ice caps, but that water has been oxygenated by eons of photosynthesis by blue-green algae. There's no simple way for that to have happened on Europa. Still, the allure is powerful: We want to find out for sure. How are we going to do it?

"The engineering problems are so titanic, NASA is smart enough to know . . . we're going to need decades of research and development," explains Dr. Stephen Gorevan, co-founder of Honeybee Robotics. "We're talking about digging a hole . . . millions of miles away, with only a small amount of power . . . half a mile deep . . . And there's no solar power available out there, so you're going to have to bring nuclear power." ∎

BACK TO BASICS

Does Salty Water Mean There's Life Down There?

Scientists generally agree that to sustain life as we know it, an ecosystem must have a steady heat source, liquid water, and a critical set of chemicals, including carbon and nitrogen compounds. Finding all three in one place, like Saturn's moon Enceladus, makes it a hot spot to look for extraterrestrial life. "[Enceladus] is exactly the kind of environment that . . . could be inhabited by living organisms," says planetary scientist Dr. Carolyn Porco. "It's watery. The salt in it tells us that the water is in contact with rocks, so there's available chemical energy for the organisms to live if they can't live off sunlight. And there's organic materials, so to me, it is the most accessible habitable zone in our solar system."

THINK ON THIS ▸ What Would Life Look Like on Titan?

Saturn's moon Titan is even larger than the planet Mercury, and it also has an atmosphere thicker than Earth's. But it's cold—its mountains are made of frozen water, and its lakes and rivers are made of liquid natural gas. If life could exist there, it could be truly exotic by Earth standards. Maybe, suggests Bill Nye the Gas Guy, it ingests hydrogen and acetylene while excreting methane.

"Welcome back to StarTalk, from Manhattan, New York City, North America, Western Hemisphere, Earth, solar system, Sagittarius Arm, Milky Way galaxy, Local Group, Virgo supercluster, the universe . . . And we don't yet have a coordinate within the multiverse—we're working on that."

—DR. NEIL DEGRASSE TYSON

CHAPTER FIVE

Are We There Yet?

We don't have to go far—just a few hundred million miles, well within our own solar system—to find all kinds of fascinating objects, structures, and materials. Not just big things, either—everything from chunks of ice, rock, and metal, from small planetlike bodies down to building-size blocks.

The vast majority of the mass in the solar system—more than 99.99 percent—resides in just 10 massive bodies. But the number of small solar system objects—at least 10,000 at last count (and that's probably less than one percent of what's out there)—far outstrips the number of big planets and moons. That's plenty of new places to examine and explore, right?

Our first explorations of these small solar system bodies may bring opportunity! Many of the first voyagers to the "New" World set out to seek fortunes. In the same way, discovery and exploitation of what's out there in the solar system could bring economic wealth. How will that change the "Old" World we live on now?

Astronomers use a metric called the cosmic distance ladder to measure the expansion rate of the universe.

Why Is Kepler-37b a Planet, but Pluto Is Not?

Well, rigorously speaking, Kepler-37b is an exoplanet and Pluto is a dwarf planet—so they're both sorta-kinda planets and both sorta-kinda not.

▲ MARS

The red planet has a radius of 2,110 miles—about half the diameter of Earth. Mars is a cold desert planet, but much like Earth it has seasons, volcanoes, and varying weather. However, Martian gravity is only 38 percent of that on Earth, and its atmosphere is too thin to sustain liquid water on its surface.

▲ EARTH

Our home planet has a radius of 3,960 miles and is the only planet in our solar system that we know of to host life. Earth orbits the Sun—at a distance of 93 million miles—and scientists have measured its age to be more than 4.5 billion years.

▲ KEPLER-37D

Discovered with the Kepler Space Telescope, Kepler-37d is the largest of the three known exoplanets orbiting the star Kepler-37. It is twice the diameter of Earth and orbits its star every 40 days.

Cosmic Queries: Tour of the Solar System

How Is Jupiter the Solar System's Vacuum Cleaner?

The biggest planet in our solar system, Jupiter takes care of us. Neil explains how: "Jupiter has more mass than everything else known that orbits the Sun. So, if you're a comet coming from far out in the solar system and you're aiming towards Earth, you've got to get past Jupiter. And here's your trajectory, with Earth in your sights, and Jupiter says, 'Uh-uh. First, I want you to hit me.' And Jupiter can eat a comet like it's nobody's business.

"Others will come in, try to get past Jupiter unscathed, and they won't—Jupiter will swing the thing around, do-si-do, and cast it back out to the solar system so it never even makes it to the Sun. And in other cases, it can swing around Jupiter and be flung out of the solar system entirely.

"[Jupiter] is our big brother protecting us from the hazards of the outer solar system . . . If it weren't for Jupiter, you can justifiably question whether Earth could have ever made it from simple life to complex life." ∎

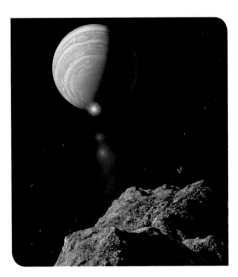

Comet Shoemaker-Levy 9 on a collision course with Jupiter

BACK TO BASICS

Where Did Saturn's E Ring Come From?

So far, in the 21st century we've discovered two rings of Saturn well beyond those ordinarily visible with a small telescope from Earth. And one of those rings happens to have one of Saturn's most interesting moons orbiting within it: "That beautiful blue E ring . . . is created by a hundred geysers erupting from the south polar terrain of a tiny moon called Enceladus, which is no bigger across than Great Britain," planetary scientist Dr. Carolyn Porco says. "Those geysers, we are virtually certain, erupt from a layer of salty liquid water laced with organic materials and bathed in excess heat."

LAUGH OUT LOUD ▶ **With Dr. Neil deGrasse Tyson, Astro-Tub-Icist**

"Saturn's density is so low because it has so much gas in it that . . . if you scooped out an average piece, it would float on water. And when I was a kid, I wanted a rubber Saturn instead of a rubber ducky—because I knew Saturn floated—to play with in my tub. But no one made it."

Where Do Comets Come From?

Astronomers divide comets into two general categories—short-period comets, which take less than a couple of centuries to orbit the Sun, and long-period comets, which take more. Most short-period comets reside in the Kuiper belt—a doughnut-shaped zone beyond the orbit of Neptune, centered on the Sun, that also contains Pluto, Eris, and several other dwarf planets that are essentially really big comets.

Most long-period comets reside in the Oort cloud (named after the Dutch astrophysicist Jan Hendrik Oort), a huge spherical shell also centered on the Sun. It may be a trillion miles across and may contain many trillions of comets. A very tiny percentage of Oort cloud objects ever make it to the inner solar system.

Taking this question in a more existential direction—that is, how do comets come into existence?—we face a big cosmic mystery. We know comets are made of ice and dust, but how did scads of little bits of matter come together in deep space to make these distant, isolated solid chunks?

"Comets and some other asteroids might be rubble piles, just rocks that are gathered together," Neil tells us. "It's porous, or it's just a pile of rubble traveling together, pretending it's one solid object." ∎

> "It was not until recently that we had any clue what the structural integrity of comets or asteroids actually is . ... We don't really know how tightly held together these things are."
>
> —DR. NEIL DEGRASSE TYSON

Comet McNaught blazed across Australia's lower Eyre Peninsula in 2007.

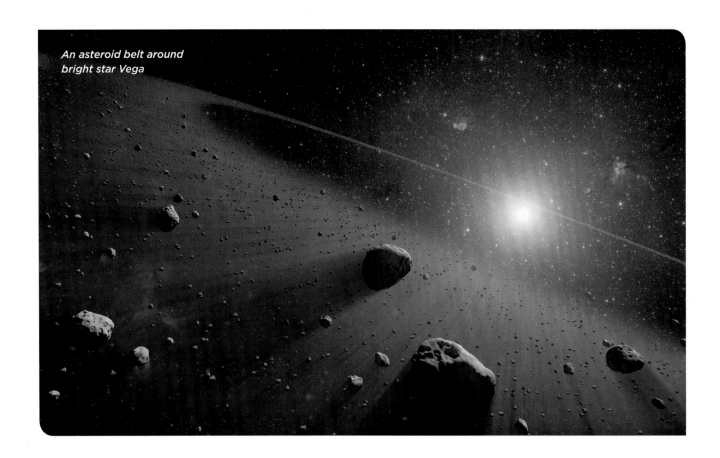

An asteroid belt around bright star Vega

How Did the Asteroid Belt Get There?

"Asteroids and comets are kind of like the leftover bits of junk that were the remnants of what happened when our solar system first formed about 4.5 billion years ago," explains astrophysicist Dr. Amy Mainzer. "Those little bits of space debris are what became the asteroids and the comets today. Things that formed a little further away from the Sun, where it was cold and really dark—those formed the comets, the icy stuff. And the stuff that formed closer to the middle, the rockier stuff that formed where it was too hot for ice— that's how you get asteroids." ◼

▶ **HOW MUCH MASS IS IN THE ASTEROID BELT?**

"Bring all the asteroid pieces together, and they will sum up to about 5 percent of the mass of our moon." —Dr. Neil deGrasse Tyson, asteroid-icist

5%

DID YOU KNOW
Astronomers think much of Earth's
oceans could have been formed
by comets striking our planet
and depositing their water
on Earth's surface.

Can I Buy and Own an Asteroid?

"If you can't have ownership, no one's going to go out there and extract the materials, and the loser is humanity."
—DR. PETER DIAMANDIS, CO-FOUNDER OF PLANETARY RESOURCES

International law about the ownership of nonterrestrial property is not yet mature. As of 2015, there exists an agreement—the Agreement Governing the Activities of States on the Moon and Other Celestial Bodies (the "Moon Treaty")—but the United States and most other spacefaring nations have not ratified it. Meanwhile, on November 25, 2015, President Barack Obama signed into law the U.S. Commercial Space Launch Competitiveness Act, under which U.S. citizens can own any asteroid resources they obtain.

"Not owning the Moon, I can agree with. But owning a 10-meter rock in space? I mean, where do you draw the line?"
—DR. PETER DIAMANDIS, CO-FOUNDER OF PLANETARY RESOURCES

At least one U.S. company—Planetary Resources—plans to launch space telescopes specifically designed to assess the commercial values of near-Earth asteroids. If their research shows that exploiting an asteroid would be profitable, they will likely chase down and capture the asteroid with rockets, claim it, and start mining it. ■

Asteroids are particularly alluring to prospectors.

DID YOU KNOW

Metallic asteroids are often rich in palladium, platinum, rhodium, and other very valuable elements important for use in batteries, electronics, and medical technology.

THINK ON THIS ▶ Why Are Some Asteroids Metal-Rich?

Gravity works inside large planetoids, causing denser metals to sink to the center to form a metal-rich core. "Then another object smashes it to smithereens, and the smithereens are now asteroids," astro-metallurgist Dr. Neil deGrasse Tyson explains. "So now you have rocky asteroids made from the crust and mantle of that object, and then you have metallic asteroids, the precious few atoms that collected in the center. Geologists call this differentiation."

Asteroid, Dwarf Planet, or Both?

Right now, Ceres is both the largest asteroid and the smallest dwarf planet.
In life, lots of things occupy two or more classifications,
so why not solar system objects?
That doesn't mean everyone has to agree, though.

|||||||
▶ DWARF PLANET

If a solar system object is
roughly round and also orbits
the Sun as its primary, but is
not by far the largest object
in its orbital path, then the
International Astronomical
Union can declare it to be a
dwarf planet, like Pluto.

|||||||
▲ METEORITE

If an object falls to Earth
from space and solid pieces
survive, these pieces are
called meteorites. More than
90 percent of meteorites
are mostly stony; only a
few are mostly metallic.

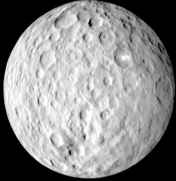

|||||||
◀ CERES

Ceres is the first minor planet
to be discovered, with a
diameter of about 590 miles.
It's the only dwarf planet in
the asteroid belt, found
between the orbits of Mars
and Jupiter.

|||||||
▶ METEOR

These are "shooting stars"
—objects that burn up in
Earth's atmosphere as
they fall, leaving an ethereal
streak of light. Most meteors
are the size of a grain of sand.

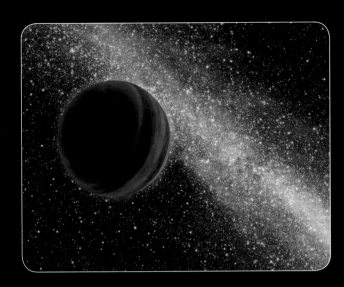

||||||
◀ ROGUE PLANET

Theoretically, a planet can be ejected from its original solar system by a gravitational "kick" and fly through interstellar space without a sun. Astronomers haven't seen one yet, though.

||||||
▶ ASTEROID

The name means "starlike" —but asteroids are actually more planetlike, just a little small. Tumbling through space as they orbit, even small ones seem to show significant geological activity.

||||||
◀ COMET

These icy dirtballs of the solar system melt away as they approach the Sun, leaving tails of both dust particles and charged ions blown into beautiful arcs by the solar wind.

Our solar system is littered with asteroids and comets.

Can We Catch a Ride on a Comet or Asteroid and Travel the Stars?

"It sounds like a really cool idea, because asteroids are going everywhere. But the physics prevents that from being a useful idea."

—DR. NEIL DEGRASSE TYSON

Wouldn't it be great if hitchhikers really could hop on an asteroid and tour the galaxy? Unfortunately, Neil can tell us why we can't just go ahead and do that: "It *so* would not work, because you would have to catch up with the asteroid to step onto it, and by the time you've done that, you're already in motion."

Or, as comedian Chuck Nice puts it: "It's like driving a Ferrari to catch a bus."

Exactly! "If you have the Ferrari, you don't need the bus," says Neil. "Now if you somehow found a way to get the asteroid to stop and start, but whatever power that is, if you've got it, you don't need the asteroid. You've got your own spaceship."

Riding an asteroid wouldn't be so bad: You'd have enough room to build a comfy home, mine it for its valuable minerals, and maybe even grow food on it. But you'd have to get on first—and then it'd have to escape the Sun's gravity to get you to the stars. ■

Are There Asteroids That Act Like Comets?

Some asteroids act like comets, and some comets act like asteroids. And some astrophysicists, like Dr. Amy Mainzer, will argue the night away about exactly how those objects should be classified: "It's kind of a continuum . . . We used to think that they were two totally different things, and now we know that there's a gray area in between . . . Sometimes we have asteroids who are, well, 'Sometimes we emit lots of gas and have comas that come off of us.' . . . They are basically things that can sometimes cross the boundaries between asteroids and comets." The best-known objects that behave ambiguously, like a half asteroid and half comet, are the Centaurs, a class of objects aptly named for the mythical creatures that were half man and half horse. Centaurs (the space objects) orbit primarily between the main asteroid belt and the Kuiper belt, and seem to be mixtures of ice, rock, and metal. The largest Centaurs are more than 100 miles across—way bigger than most comets.

They're not rare, either; more than 300 Centaurs have been catalogued, and planetary scientists estimate there are at least 40,000 of them. ■

> *"Astronomers are going to be fighting about this for many decades to come . . . Astronomers are normally pretty quiet people, but not when it comes to this stuff."*
>
> —DR. AMY MAINZER, ASTROPHYSICIST

TOUR GUIDE

What's the Coolest Asteroid?

Asteroid 2010 TK7, discovered in 2011 with the WISE spacecraft. At least according to astrophysicist Dr. Amy Mainzer: "It's called the first-known Earth Trojan, and this is an asteroid that's stuck to the Earth in a peculiar way. It is actually trapped in a gravitational resonance with the Earth, which sounds really cool, and [it means that] Earth is following it around in its orbit around the Sun. It's kind of trapped there, and what's going to happen is, eventually, it's going to pop its way out."

DID YOU KNOW
Every 2,000 years or so, a meteoroid the size of a football field hits Earth and causes significant damage.

THINK ON THIS ▶ **Why Did Comet ISON Fizzle?**

"[Comets] just do whatever they feel like . . . They are exactly like teenagers, or cats . . . We just recently had a so-called 'comet of the century' called comet ISON. It wasn't just a dud. It was a nothing . . . We were really hoping it would come back and make this great fireworks show, and nothing. Just like cats."
—Dr. Amy Mainzer, astrophysicist

PLANET EARTH

||||||||||||||||||||||||||||||||||||||||||

Earth is a little ball of mud orbiting a little ball of gas
in a big, big universe. Oh, but what a ball of mud it is!
Thanks to billions of years of continual change, our planet
is the perfect place for us to have come of age in the
cosmos—and now, to start our journey to the stars. What
do we actually know about Earth? How should we utilize
it and take care of it—and, at the same time, ourselves?
The more we learn, the better we can do.

"The thought that went through my head was, This must be the view from heaven. But it was replaced by a thought right after, which was, No, no, it's more beautiful than that. This is what heaven must look like."

—DR. MIKE MASSIMINO, ASTRONAUT

CHAPTER ONE

Pale Blue Dot or Big Blue Marble?

Earth is just one world among many in our solar system. Not that long ago, we humans finally began to understand where we are in space: We orbit a star, the Sun, and we're orbited by one natural satellite, the Moon. Knowledge of how Earth behaves, moves, and interacts with other bodies in the solar system has brought humans an awareness of our cosmic neighborhood and our neighbors in it.

We were built from Earth, by Earth, and we have evolved side by side with Earth for billions of years, from our first cellular ancestors to the modern junk-food muncher. When we learn about Earth's origins, we're learning about our own beginnings, and when we see natural phenomena, we build technology to study them—and learn more about ourselves in the process.

Earth is both a pale blue dot in space and a big blue marble full of beauty and majesty. It's only natural, when contemplating our planet, to think deeply and grandly about our place in the cosmos.

*Set inside a marble, it's easy to
see Earth in a brand-new light.*

So What Is Earth, Exactly?

Can a goldfish truly understand its bowl without taking a look from the outside? We use our eyes and our machines to look to the stars, but when we peer back at ourselves, this is what we see.

||||||
◀ "BLUE MARBLE"

The original "Blue Marble" photograph was taken from Apollo 17 on December 7, 1972, at a distance of 28,000 miles from Earth.

||||||
▶ EARTH'S HORIZON

An Expedition 7 crew member on board the ISS in July 2003 captured this view of Earth's horizon as the Sun set over the Pacific Ocean.

Earth

||||||
◀ "THE DAY THE EARTH SMILED"

Earth is in the background of a photograph of Saturn, taken from Cassini on July 19, 2013, at a distance of 900 million miles.

IIIIIII
▶ "EARTHRISE"

Declared "the most influential environmental photo ever taken," "Earthrise" was shot from Apollo 8 on December 24, 1968, from a distance of 240,000 miles.

IIIIIII
◀ "PALE BLUE DOT"

Transmitted from Voyager 1, the "Pale Blue Dot" photograph of Earth was shot on February 14, 1990, at a distance of 3.76 billion miles.

IIIIIII
▶ EARTH AT NIGHT

Perhaps more than any other images, pictures like these confirm the presence of humanity on our planet. Extraterrestrial visitors, seeing the light we make in the dark, would have no doubt we are here.

The famous "Earthrise" picture was taken by astronauts on Apollo 8.

How Did Apollo 8 and "Earthrise" Influence the Environmental Movement?

"We went to the Moon, looking to discover it, and we looked back and we discovered Earth for the first time."

—DR. NEIL DEGRASSE TYSON

Today, we hardly think anything of the pictures of Earth taken from space. After all, you can see them on every TV weather report. Before the Apollo era, though, an image like that was unthinkable.

On Christmas Eve in 1968, astronaut William Anders and his Apollo 8 crewmates held a historic live-from-space broadcast that showed pictures of Earth and the Moon viewed from their spacecraft. Upon their return, "Earthrise" (above) became one of the most iconic images in history. For the first time, the people of the world were able to appreciate Earth as a whole, from afar—beautiful, isolated, and fragile.

The environmental movement in the United States was young then, having started in earnest in 1962 with marine biologist Rachel Carson's book *Silent Spring,* which warned of the dangers of pesticide overuse. But "Earthrise" cemented the realization that our planet's environment needed help. Two years after Apollo 8, on December 2, 1970, President Richard Nixon approved the establishment of the Environmental Protection Agency. ■

Madame Saturn: A Conversation With Carolyn Porco (Part 2)

The Day the Earth Smiled

Two decades after "Pale Blue Dot," that iconic Voyager 1 picture of Earth, was taken, planetary scientist Carolyn Porco was the leader of the imaging team for Cassini-Huygens, a multiyear mission to Saturn and its moons. Why not get a new portrait of our planet? she thought. Here's how she recalls the day: "The 15 minutes that it was happening and I'm looking where Saturn is; and I'm thinking, Wow, there's a camera there taking our picture; and knowing that people all over the world were doing the same thing—it was fabulous."

Her plan was to tell everyone on Earth what was happening, to be ready for it, and to say "Cheese!" for the spacecraft's camera. On July 19, 2013, that's exactly what happened. "And I'm thinking, Why don't we tell people in advance: 'Your picture is going to be taken from the outer solar system, from a billion miles away' . . . How better to let them know how far humans have come in the exploration of the solar system," she recalls. "It becomes something personal to them . . . because the idea was to smile in celebration. To get this communal feeling out of people, this kind of cosmic love . . . And one person wrote, 'You know, darn it, we may be floating around on a dust mote, we may be transient, but for 15 minutes, we were there, we were aware, and we smiled.' " ∎

"The Day the Earth Smiled" is re-created from a collage of 1,600 images submitted to NASA's "Wave at Saturn" campaign.

BIOGRAPHY

👓

Carl Sagan and the Spirituality of Space

Carl Sagan (1934–1996) was the foremost science communicator of the 20th century—but not just because he was a top scientist who could explain his research clearly. Sagan helped people connect with science in every context; whether it was technical, practical, hypothetical, or even spiritual, he showed everyone how the universe related to them. Sagan was Jewish, but his sense of the cosmic transcended any single faith tradition. As he wrote in his 1994 book, *Pale Blue Dot,* about the tiny image of Earth from Voyager 1: "The aggregate of our joy and suffering, thousands of confident religions, ideologies and economic doctrines . . . every teacher of morals, every corrupt politician, every 'superstar,' every 'supreme leader,' every saint and sinner in the history of our species, lived there on a mote of dust suspended in a sunbeam."

Cosmic Queries: Planet Earth

How Was Earth Formed?

About 4.6 billion years ago, soon after nuclear fusion in the Sun began, the leftover material from the Sun's formation settled into a thin disk rotating around our infant star. This disk contained enough bits of rock, metal, dust, and gas to make hundreds of Earths; and over millions of years, in a process called accretion, the bits came together to build pebbles, then rocks, then boulders, then planetesimals, then planetoids—and then, finally, planets.

NEIL: *If you don't have enough gravity to begin with, you hold your rocks; you don't hold your gas.*

CHUCK NICE: *You mean Uranus is gassy?*

Earth formed in a region of the solar system where there wasn't a whole lot of material, and what was there consisted mostly of rock and metal. That's why our planet is small, solid, and rocky-metallic—a terrestrial planet like Mercury, Venus, and Mars. Jupiter, Saturn, Uranus, and Neptune, on the other hand, formed where there was much more planet-building raw material, but it was mostly gas and almost no metal, and so they became gas giant planets with cores of rock and ice.

This simple picture of planetary formation is hardly the whole scientific story, of course. Lots of mysteries remain. For example: Zipping around the Sun at thousands of miles an hour, the original bits of matter probably bounced off one another, so how did they join to form larger bodies? There is plenty left to learn! ■

BACK TO BASICS

What Was the Greatest Wrong Idea Ever?

"There's nothing wrong with a wrong idea," says Dr. Neil deGrasse Tyson, astro-wrong-icist. "[As long as] it helps you try to solve a problem. One of the greatest wrong ideas ever was the geocentric universe, with the Earth in the middle."

The geocentric model of the universe was proven to be spectacularly incorrect—yet it helped explain how things move in the universe as viewed from Earth. Even more importantly, the people who codified geocentrism—Aristotle, Ptolemy, and other great thinkers—created a model that could be tested scientifically, and that allowed their descendants to keep improving humanity's view of the cosmos.

THINK ON THIS ▸ How Did Our Sun Form?

Nearly five billion years ago, a dense core of gas collected in a vast interstellar cloud trillions of miles across. That cloud collapsed in on itself, creating a core with a temperature of more than 20,000,000°F and pressure two billion times that of Earth's atmosphere—nearly 30 billion pounds per square inch—conditions extreme enough to induce hydrogen to fuse into helium. Then the collapse halted, and the Sun was born.

Where Do Earth's Heavy Metals Come From?

You don't get the real answer to Neil's question until you study astrophysics and ask again, Where do these elements come from? "They are cooked in the crucibles of high-mass stars, forged from small elements like hydrogen and helium; they are fused together to make high-mass elements, and they ride their way up the periodic table of elements," explains astro-chemi-cist Dr. Neil deGrasse Tyson. "And then that same star explodes, scattering its guts into the galaxy, out of which you make subsequent solar systems."

The astrophysicist's answer to this question shows how we're connected to the entire universe at literally

"When I was a kid in chemistry class, I'd ask the chemistry teacher, 'Where do these elements come from, that sit up there on the periodic table?' 'We find them in the ground.' That was the chemistry teacher's answer."

—DR. NEIL DEGRASSE TYSON, ASTRO-TEEN-ICIST

the atomic level. When stars much more massive than our Sun explode as supernovae, atomic nuclei and subatomic particles crash into one another in super-high-energy interactions, and heavy elements are created in a fraction of a second. This is "rapid-process nucleosynthesis," which produces most of the heavy elements in the universe.

Stars that don't explode, like our Sun, can also produce heavy elements during a short period of their lifetimes, when they swell in size to become giants. This is "slow-process nucleosynthesis," which takes thousands of years. Some elements can only be made by one process, while others can be produced by either. ■

A marble statue of Atlas, the Greek god of astronomy and navigation, bearing the weight of Earth on his shoulders

YouTube: Neil deGrasse Tyson on Lunar Phases and Tides

Does the Full Moon Make Earth's Tides Stronger?

The Moon is the main reason why oceans have tides: The Moon's gravity has a stronger influence on the side of Earth nearest to it, and it draws Earth's water toward it ever so slightly, which causes daily tides. Maybe you have noticed that tides run higher during a full moon—but it's not the Moon's phase that causes that. The Moon's tidal effects depend only on its mass and distance from Earth, which stay almost constant no matter what its phase.

So what makes high tides get even higher? It has to do with the Sun. The Sun also has a gravitational pull on Earth, although a little less than half that of the Moon. A full moon happens when the Sun lines up with Earth and the Moon, and in that position, the Sun adds its gravitational influence on our oceans. Those higher-than-high tides are called spring tides, because the water seems to "spring" upward just a little more than usual. Between the full and new moon, during the quarter phases, the Sun pulls at right angles to the Moon's pull, creating a weaker result and relatively lower high tides, called neap tides. ∎

> *"Why do we have a higher tide during full moon? Because the Sun's tides add to the Moon's tides. It's the Sun. Blame the Sun."*
>
> —DR. NEIL DEGRASSE TYSON, ASTRO-SUN-ICIST

TOUR GUIDE

What's the Deal With the "Super Moon"?

Now and then, the buzz goes around: Watch for the super moon tonight. So what's a super moon? Don't get astro-moon-icist Dr. Neil deGrasse Tyson started: "I don't know who first called it a super moon. But if you have a 16-inch pizza, would you call it a super pizza compared to a 15-inch pizza? The Moon's orbit around the Earth is not a perfect circle. Sometimes it's closer; sometimes it's farther away. And every month, there's a moment when it's closest. Occasionally, that moment coincides with a full moon. People are calling that a super moon. But there are super half-moons. Every month, every one of the phases is the closest. I don't hear people say, 'Oh, cool, super crescent.' I told you, don't get me started."

THINK ON THIS ▶ Why Is the Moon Short on Iron?

A much lower percentage of the Moon's mass is iron compared with Earth's, yet the Moon and Earth have nearly identical crusts. Astronomers think that's because a Mars-size planet crashed into Earth billions of years ago, throwing a lot of rock into orbit, but not a lot of metal. That rocky material eventually formed the Moon.

Meltwater pools on the Greenland Ice Sheet may influence Earth's rotation.

Cosmic Queries: Planet Earth

How Do Earthquakes and Melting Glaciers Change Earth's Rotation?

HOW MUCH DOES EARTH WEIGH?

"You could justifiably say the Earth is weightless in space," says Neil. Its mass, on the other hand, is about six billion trillion tons.

Rotating bodies, be they planets or people, follow a fundamental law called conservation of angular momentum. As Neil explains it: "Skaters do this when they pull their arms in—they are changing their own moment of inertia. What happens to their rotation rate? They go faster. And how do they stop? They put their arms back out, and they can stop on a dime. So they change their own rotation rate by bringing their arms in or out."

The December 2004 earthquake in the Indian Ocean, the third strongest ever recorded, shortened the length of our day by an estimated two microseconds. Melting glaciers, on the other hand, increase Earth's diameter by creating higher sea levels, lengthening the day by about a thousandth of a second since the year 1900. Think of the earthquake as the skater pulling in her arms; think of Earth with higher sea levels as the skater spreading them out. "You can calculate how much we change after every earthquake, because an earthquake is a redistribution of the continental shelf," says Neil. "In fact, melting glaciers change the rotation rate of the Earth, too." ∎

Cosmic Queries: Grab Bag

Why Do Planets Revolve Around the Sun on the Same Plane?

DID YOU KNOW

The solar system extends for billions of miles outward from the Sun, yet it contains less than one-tenth of one percent of the Sun's mass—and most of that is the planet Jupiter.

Over the course of a year, the path of the Sun across the sky traces out a surface called the ecliptic plane. All the planets move on or very close to this plane as they orbit the Sun—and they all do so traveling in the same direction. Amazing coincidence? No, there's a reason. Let Dr. Neil deGrasse Tyson, astro-pancake-ist, explain: "In the formation of the solar system, you have this huge rotating gas cloud, and it wants to collapse under its own gravity. As it collapses, it pancakes, and out of that revolving material, it makes objects. And so if you make planets out of that rotating material [as it's moving], those planets all orbit the Sun in the same direction, on the [same] plane . . . Everything's in a plane, and they're going in the same direction together." ■

> "If you come upon a solar system, and a planet is orbiting some other funky way, you can bet your . . . orbital parameters that planet was captured from another place outside your solar system."
>
> —DR. NEIL DEGRASSE TYSON

A rendering of the eight planets of our solar system on the same plane

DID YOU KNOW

According to Neil, if Earth's rotation speed suddenly doubled, the force required to make that happen would "flatten you into a pile of goo."

THINK ON THIS ▶ Why Are Days Shorter at the Winter Solstice?

Earth's polar axis slants. So as Earth orbits the Sun, sometimes the Northern Hemisphere leans more toward the Sun and sometimes it leans away. Daylight hours can vary throughout the year as a result. On the winter solstice, the North Pole is leaning farthest away from the Sun, so daylight hours are shortest—but simultaneously, the Southern Hemisphere is leaning as close toward the Sun as it ever gets, and experiences the longest day of the year.

Cosmic Queries: A Powerful Potpourri

What Happened to the Meteors?

Huge dents in Earth's crust have been made over the eons by meteors slamming into our planet. Depending on where they hit and the environmental conditions surrounding them, those craters are still visible millions of years after impact. But the rocks themselves are gone! Why?

Scientists have used computer simulations and calculations to envision such an event and solve the puzzle. When a meteor of great size strikes a solid surface at hypersonic speed, the object explodes on impact. The detonation creates a perfectly symmetrical round hole, no matter what angle the collision occurred—and there's nothing left of the meteor but vapor. ∎

Meteor Crater
A 150-foot-wide metallic meteor struck the Mogollon Rim in modern-day Arizona 50,000 years ago, leaving a mile-wide hole that's 60 stories deep.

Chesapeake Bay
A mile-wide meteor hit the Eastern Shore of the United States 35 million years ago, pushing the surrounding land downward. That indentation eventually filled with water.

Chicxulub
About 65 million years ago, a 10-mile-wide meteor pounded the planet, off the coast of modern-day Mexico's Yucatán Peninsula. Its impact on Earth's atmosphere may have led to the extinction of the dinosaurs.

"Meteor Crater was purchased by a metal speculator, because he presumed that the huge object that made the crater was still buried underneath . . . Didn't find a thing, poor guy."

—DR. NEIL DEGRASSE TYSON, ASTRO-CRATER-CIST

BACK TO BASICS

How Thick Is Earth's Atmosphere?

Gas molecules in Earth's atmosphere extend thousands of miles above sea level. Above a couple of hundred miles, though, the atmosphere is so thin that we can hardly distinguish it from the vacuum of space. So exactly how do we measure the "thickness" of Earth's—or any planet's—atmosphere? One way is to measure the pressure at the bottom of the atmosphere. On Earth, that's about 14.7 pounds of force per square inch. That means typical human adults constantly experience nearly 20 tons of force on their bodies, just from Earth's atmosphere! As impressive as that sounds, Venus has an atmosphere 90 times denser than Earth's—and the atmospheres of the gas giant planets Jupiter, Saturn, Uranus, and Neptune are thousands of times denser than that.

THINK ON THIS ▶ How Does Light Get Through the Greenhouse Effect?

Greenhouse gases keep heat from escaping the atmosphere—why don't they keep sunlight from coming in? Doesn't sunlight heat Earth? "The Sun does not heat the air," explains astro-solar-cist Dr. Neil deGrasse Tyson. The Sun heats the ground, and the ground heats the air. Visible light hits Earth and heats it. Earth reradiates that same energy as infrared, and it's the infrared that gets trapped by the greenhouse gases."

Carved channels on Mars may indicate the planet once had surface water.

What Can We Learn About Earth From Venus and Mars?

Was Venus once Earthlike?

Venus and Mars have undergone climate changes that dwarf any earthly scale—and have mighty stories to tell. Says astrobiologist Dr. David Grinspoon about Venus: "Venus started off Earthlike. As near as we can tell, it did have oceans and water and was cooler when it was young, and then as the Sun heated up . . . it passed a point where things got hot enough, so the oceans started to evaporate. As the oceans evaporated, there was more water vapor in the air. Water vapor is a strong greenhouse gas, so water vapor in the air makes it hotter at the surface, which leads to more evaporation of the oceans, more greenhouse gas in the atmosphere. It's a positive feedback—it runs away. It got to the point where the oceans literally boiled off."

Mars experienced a greenhouse effect that didn't run away—it ran out. Billions of years ago, Mars probably had liquid water on its surface, but things got too cold, and the atmosphere dissipated into space. Martian oceans either evaporated or froze solid deep underground. ■

YouTube: Neil deGrasse Tyson Explains the Aurora Borealis

What Causes an Aurora Borealis?

In addition to light, electrically charged subatomic particles stream outward from the Sun into the solar system. Given time, these particles would damage living tissue and render Earth uninhabitable. Fortunately for us, Earth generates a magnetic field as it spins, and this field directs most of these charged particles away from Earth's surface and harmlessly into space.

Sometimes, the number of charged particles spikes upward—for example, if the Sun has a solar flare or a coronal mass ejection. The extra particle flux streams along Earth's magnetic field lines toward the magnetic pole, crashing into the molecules of our upper atmosphere. The resulting release of energy is the cosmic light show known as the northern lights, or the aurora borealis. When it happens in the Southern Hemisphere, it's called—you guessed it—the southern lights, or the aurora australis.

Auroras are especially beautiful when viewed from space—where they appear as flowing rivers of eerie light cascading downward toward Earth's surface. We see them, sometimes spectacularly, around other planets, too. ◼

A vivid aurora borealis over Russia

BACK TO BASICS

Why Do Stars Twinkle?

Even on the calmest days, the air in Earth's atmosphere jiggles and shimmies. Twinkling happens when the light from a distant point travels through that atmosphere; its light beam dances ever so slightly in random directions many times—sometimes thousands of times—each second. To an astronomer on Earth, looking at a distant star through the atmosphere is like looking up at a firefly from the bottom of a swimming pool. That's why telescopes in space are so important—they rise above the obscuring effects of the atmosphere and send down images with clarity unobtainable on terra firma.

"'Twinkle, twinkle, little star, how I wonder what you are' is the bane of all modern astronomy, because the twinkling is atmospheric."

—DR. NEIL DEGRASSE TYSON, ASTRO-MUSICOLOGIST

The Past, Present & Future of Space Telescopes?

From Galileo's handheld device to today's orbiting marvels, telescopes revolutionize our understanding of who we are. "Every time you turn a bigger telescope to the night sky, we end up smaller than we had previously imagined . . . It is an ego-dismantling device," says Neil.

||||||||
◀ GALILEO'S TELESCOPE

This wooden tube containing two lenses gave Galileo Galilei barely 20 times the light-gathering power of unaided eyes—and revealed that Earth was just a planet in a whirling Sun-centered solar system.

100" Reflecting Telescope Mt. Wilson Calif.

||||||||
◀ HOOKER TELESCOPE

With this telescope, located at Mount Wilson Observatory (above) in California and powered by a mirror 100 inches across, Edwin Hubble discovered that ours is but one galaxy among billions in the universe.

||||||||
◀ HALE TELESCOPE

By many measures the most productive telescope in history, this iconic 200-inch telescope on Mount Palomar in California brought astronomy into the modern era of observational cosmology.

ARECIBO OBSERVATORY

This radio telescope, 1,000 feet across and larger than 25 football fields, was built into a natural valley in Puerto Rico. Its many uses include listening for signs of extraterrestrial intelligence.

|||||||

▶ KECK TELESCOPES

Sitting 14,000 feet above sea level at an observatory on Mauna Kea in Hawaii, the twin Keck I and Keck II telescopes each combine 36 hexagonal mirrors into a single light-gathering surface nearly 400 inches across.

|||||||

◀ HUBBLE SPACE TELESCOPE

The most important scientific instrument of its generation, Hubble has been upgraded five times by astronauts tending it from orbiting space vehicles. Today it's about 100 times more powerful than when it was launched a quarter century ago.

|||||||

▲ CHANDRA X-RAY OBSERVATORY

CXO is sensitive to light that would never reach Earth's surface and that human eyes can't detect. With optics specially positioned to catch x-rays, it almost looks as if it's pointed backward.

|||||||

KEPLER SPACE TELESCOPE

Named after the astronomer who discovered the elliptical orbits of planets, this special-purpose space telescope has been used to find thousands of planets so far—all of them orbiting stars other than the Sun.

|||||||

▼ JAMES WEBB SPACE TELESCOPE

The scientific successor to the Hubble and Spitzer Space Telescopes, JWST will be sensitive to both optical and infrared light. Its adaptive optics will be able to pick out infant galaxies as well as planets orbiting distant stars.

"So you want to talk about spirituality, you take a swig of water . . . It contains water molecules that have passed through the kidneys of Abraham Lincoln, of Genghis Khan, of Jesus . . . "

—DR. NEIL DEGRASSE TYSON

CHAPTER TWO

How Do We Get Water?

Water is an amazing substance—yet it's so ubiquitous, we almost take it for granted. It's just two hydrogen atoms attached to an oxygen atom, forming a wide V-shaped structure. That shape allows water to dissolve more substances than almost any other known liquid and yet stay stable for eons without denaturing or dissipating.

Water's such a good solvent, though, that impurities, microbes, or even poisons can easily get into it as it travels. So when we get water for daily use, we sometimes have to bring it from far-away places to be sure it's clean. Constant vigilance to protect our water supplies is a must for our well-being—but with a swelling population and ever intensifying competition for living space and resources, that's getting harder and harder.

What if we don't have enough water? Or what if the water is plentiful but it's dirty or salty? Can we get more from the cosmos? After all, that's where all of our water came from, a long time ago.

The abundant water on our planet makes Earth unique.

Pilgrims bathe in the Narmada's 160-foot-tall Kadil Dhara waterfall.

Comets and Asteroids With Dr. Amy Mainzer

Where Does Our Water Come From?

"Early on, when the solar system was first forming, we do think there was a period when the Earth pretty much got pelted by asteroids and comets, and that could have been when the water got here."

—DR. AMY MAINZER, ASTROPHYSICIST

Most of Earth's water is locked in rock. You can't tell from touching it, for example, but up to a quarter of the volume of a block of sandstone could be water. For some volcanic rock and limestone, that fraction can go up to half. The amount of water in Earth's outermost layers—the crust and upper mantle—is estimated to be more than 10 times the total on Earth's surface. Early in Earth's geological history, over hundreds of millions of years, water was carried to the surface, most likely by volcanoes, and produced our oceans, lakes, and rivers.

So how did the water get there in the first place? For that, we have to look to the universe—because that's where all of Earth's building blocks came from, billions of years ago. ■

Where Have All the Comets Gone?

"Not all water is created equal."
—DR. NEIL DEGRASSE TYSON

I f the water molecules on Earth arrived here in comets, those original icy dirtballs melted long ago. But there are still comets in our solar system that can help us test this hypothesis, by comparing the atomic properties of today's water with the properties of today's comets.

So did water arrive in comets? Maybe, maybe not says astro-ocean-ist Dr. Neil deGrasse Tyson: "We checked some comets, and we noticed the water in those comets doesn't match the water in our oceans, and that got us worried . . . But then we did find a couple of comets that did match the oceans. The jury is still out, just so you know, [about] the origin of Earth's water. We know at least some came from volcanoes, and we're pretty sure there's a class of comet that did not supply the water, and other classes of comets that might."

Another point to consider: About one-half of one percent of Earth's mass is water, and about one-tenth of that water is in Earth's oceans. Just to fill the oceans, at least one billion good-size comets would be required. So there's a lot of our planet's water supply that remains unexplored, untested, and unexplained. ■

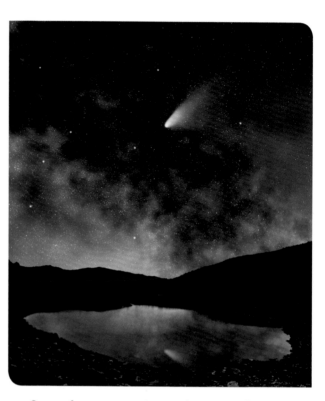
Some of our ocean water may have come from comets.

DID YOU KNOW
If the Chicxulub impactor, which may have wiped out the dinosaurs 65 million years ago, was indeed a comet, it would have deposited enough water on Earth's surface to flood the state of Florida to a depth of 10 feet.

THINK ON THIS ▶ Are Comet Water and Asteroid Water Different?
"Water is not in asteroids the way you find water in a comet. A comet [has] huge chunks of ice, and you can just carve out a piece and there it is. [In an asteroid,] water is sort of blended in with the minerals, so you actually have to extract it. You actually have to mine the water."
—Dr. Neil deGrasse Tyson

"It turns out that the Moon wasn't this dry body in the sky that we thought it was, because the Moon and Earth share a history."

—DR. YVONNE PENDLETON, DIRECTOR OF NASA'S SSERVI

StarTalk Live! From SF Sketchfest 2015

What's Wetter: Europa, Mars, or the Moon?

Jupiter's moon Europa has a crust made of ice that looks almost exactly like Earth's polar ice cap. That's led astronomers to conclude there is a lot of water deep under Europa's surface. We have yet to see one drop up top, though.

On the other hand, it's been proven that Mars has oceans of ice beneath its surface—and once in a while, that ice even appears as liquid water on the Martian surface. Warm weather can cause water to ooze out of Martian mountain walls and run downhill until it evaporates, leaving trails of mineral deposits for our orbiting telescopes to see.

It looks like there may be some water on the Moon, too, possibly in the form of ice preserved in shady craters, or chemically bound in rocky material blasted into space from a water-rich Earth four billion years ago. "Apollo astronauts picked up rock samples, and later we were able to find out there was quite a bit of water in those rocks," says Dr. Yvonne Pendleton, director of NASA's SSERVI. "The Earth was probably wet at the time when that big Mars-size object hit the Earth and created the Moon. Some of that water went to the Moon." ■

BACK TO BASICS

How Did the Moon Get Water?

Here are three ways scientists think water could have wound up on the Moon:

1. When the Moon was formed, billions of years ago, water-rich rock could have come from the infant Earth.

2. Bombardment of the Moon by comets or meteorites could have deposited water.

3. Charged particles from the Sun's solar wind could have created water molecules in the Moon's minerals.

"By the way, if you're a comet and you hit the Earth, all of your water vaporizes on contact so you would become steam, and you would have to condense back out later."

—DR. NEIL DEGRASSE TYSON, ASTRO-STEAM-ICIST

THINK ON THIS ▶ Ice, Water, and Steam: Happy Together?

Parts of Mars's surface is very close to the triple point of water, when it can be solid, liquid, and steam at the same time. That happens at 32°F and a pressure of 0.006 Earth atmosphere. "A bucket of it would just be happy having ice cubes and water, and that water will be boiling [and] creating steam," says Neil. "And the ice and the boiling water are just fine, and the boiling water doesn't melt the ice."

What Are Water's Secrets?

magine dropping an ice cube into a steaming cup of hot tea. There you have water in all three phases—solid (ice), liquid (tea), and vapor (steam)—each in the vicinity of one another. The surfaces between those phases interact in weird ways that still aren't fully understood scientifically.

When you slip on ice, what's happening? The physics of surfaces—solid or liquid, sandpaper or ice—is surprisingly complex. What we do know is that ice creates very little friction when its surface touches another solid surface. One

"Frozen water is less dense than liquid water . . . and ice floats. In the winter, the top surface [of a lake] gets cold. The top water will freeze, and not drop, thereby insulating the liquid water below, protecting the fishes through the winter months. It's a remarkable feature of water."

—DR. NEIL DEGRASSE TYSON, ASTRO-ANGLER-IST

common misconception is that ice skates melt the ice they run over, but no: That slipperiness is already a function of the low friction of the ice.

Why is ocean water salty? Salt starts as a chemical component of rock. Water running over rocks can dissolve the chemicals in those rocks. When all that water collects in one place, the water can evaporate away, but the salt stays behind. That happens in the oceans, of course, but also in some inland bodies of water, known for their high salinity, such as the Dead Sea and the Great Salt Lake. ∎

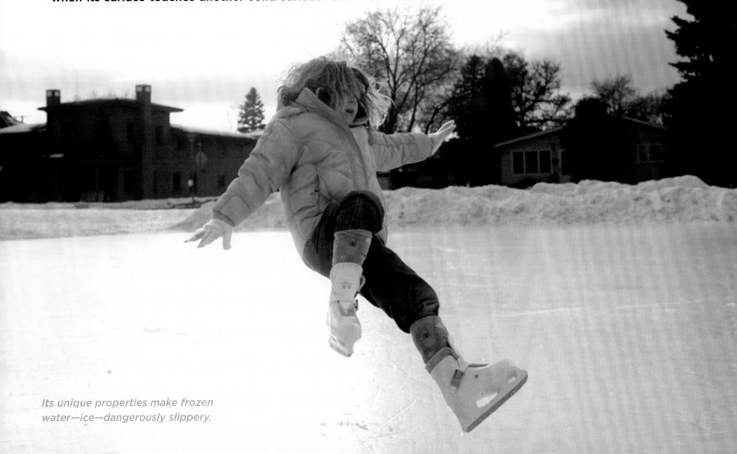

Its unique properties make frozen water—ice—dangerously slippery.

What Is the Water Cycle?

Arriving on Earth from space billions of years ago, then bubbling up onto Earth's surface through fissures and volcanoes, H_2O molecules do a perpetual dance of transformation that makes life possible.

IIIIIII
◀ EVAPORATION

Liquid water or solid ice warmed by the sun or the ground below absorbs energy and transforms into gaseous vapor. Floating into the sky, it can stream freely or collect into denser concentrations.

IIIIIII
▶ CONDENSATION

As the vapor hits chillier air, it loses heat energy and transforms back into water droplets and ice crystals. Clouds look serene from the outside, but inside there's constant swirling motion.

IIIIIII
◀ PRECIPITATION

Little bits of water and ice glom together with each other and onto bits of dust, soot, or other small particles to form raindrops and snowflakes. When they get too heavy, they fall to Earth.

|||||||
▶ INFILTRATION

Rain and liquefied snow seep into the ground through porous rock or soil. Groundwater collects. Plants suck water through their roots to use in biological processes. Animals drink.

|||||||
◀ FLOW

If too much water falls to be absorbed into the ground, the excess collects in puddles and pools. Gravity makes the water move downward toward Earth's center, creating runoff, then streams, rivers, lakes, seas, and oceans.

|||||||
▶ RETURN

Plants transpire. Animals perspire. (And, yeah, they also pee.) One particular animal—humans—uses water for everything from agriculture to industry to entertainment, and then dumps it back out into the environment. The water cycle repeats.

StarTalk Live!: Water World [Part 1]

Can I Drink Heavy Water?

Ordinary water has two hydrogen atoms and one oxygen atom: H_2O. The stuff we call heavy water has two deuterium atoms and one oxygen, and it's a little bit denser than ordinary water. Any water could have a tiny bit of heavy water in it, but to get a glass of it, you would have to start with a huge amount of water and extract the heavy water out.

Heavy water got a bad rap because of its use in developing nuclear weapons. Could you still drink it? Sure, says Neil, "You would slow down, though."

Comedian Eugene Mirman isn't buying it and asks, "Really? You wouldn't die?"

Not at all. Heavy water is made with deuterium atoms, which are actually hydrogen atoms with an extra neutron in each nucleus. So heavy water is practically identical to regular H_2O. It's not poisonous or anything. But it might not behave exactly the way you expect water to when you drink it.

Lab mice have had the experience, but we can only speculate what would happen to a human drinking heavy water. Judging by the numbers, a molecule of heavy water is 11 percent more massive than a molecule of regular water, and two-thirds of your body mass is water—so after drinking heavy water, you would be just a little heavier. ∎

Two glasses demonstrate the concept of heavy water and regular water.

DID YOU KNOW

In every million gallons of seawater, there is about three ounces of naturally occurring heavy water.

THINK ON THIS ▸ **How Much of Earth's Water Is Drinkable?**

OK, so about 0.02 percent of Earth's mass is surface water. How much of that can I drink?

DR. TESS RUSSO, GEOSCIENTIST: "About 3 percent of the water on Earth is fresh water, but most of that —two-thirds of it—is locked up in glaciers and ice."

NEIL: "So we should melt the glaciers and get more."

DR. RUSSO: "We are."

Will World War III Be About Water?

illions of people worldwide are forced to leave their homes each year because of water—either too much of it causing flooding, or too little of it causing drought and famine. "The Pentagon has done two assessments over the last decade," says Robert F. Kennedy, Jr., attorney and president of Waterkeeper Alliance, "and in both those assessments they've said that global warming, and particularly water shortages, are the principal threat to America's national security because of the disruption to global political systems and populations that it's going to cause."

High-stakes business investments come into play as well, continues Kennedy. "In the last 10 years, water privatization has become a trillion-dollar industry, according to the World Bank. We've already seen water wars fought all over the world—in Bolivia, in Cochabamba; and Belize; and many other countries where foreign companies have come in, privatized local water supplies, and then raised rates and literally killed poor people who can't afford those higher water rates."

Displaced and desperate people are much more likely to be part of civil and political strife, including crime and terrorism. Furthermore, many of the most politically sensitive places in the world, such as the Middle East, are in desert regions. Water issues can fuel violent conflict. ∎

DID YOU KNOW

In sub-Saharan Africa, most people gather their water from wells, springs, lakes, and rivers. The time spent gathering water there totals 40 billion hours a year.

If only water wars could be fought with water guns.

"There are millions of environmental refugees every year, throughout the world, who are driven off their land and who are creating civil strife, and political strife, and security problems that affect the United States because of water shortages."

—ROBERT F. KENNEDY, JR.,
ATTORNEY AND PRESIDENT OF WATERKEEPER ALLIANCE

THINK ON THIS ▸ How Much Does That Bottle of Water Really Cost?

About 50 billion plastic bottles of water are sold in the United States each year. It takes almost 20 million barrels of oil to make just the bottles, enough to keep a million cars on the road all year, or to provide electrical power to 200,000 homes. Three-fourths of these bottles aren't recycled, creating more than a billion pounds of plastic trash every single year.

Where Do We Use Water Most?

Clean water plays a huge role in modern life: drinking, bathing, housekeeping, and watering the yard and garden. The EPA estimates the average U.S. household uses 300 gallons a day. With roughly 125 million households in the country, that means we're using more than

"There are [already] a lot of technologies out there right now that if widely used would dramatically reduce the amount of water that's needed."

—ROBERT F. KENNEDY, JR., ATTORNEY AND PRESIDENT OF WATERKEEPER ALLIANCE

35 *billion* gallons of water a day.

But that's just the beginning. Households in the U.S. represent less than 10 percent of water usage. Agricultural irrigation systems and power plants each use more than four times the water that households do. Here are some of the major water users. ∎

DID YOU KNOW?

According to UNESCO, nearly one out of every nine people around the world does not have access to clean drinking water, and at least one-third of the world's population does not have the water necessary for adequate sanitation. As the world population bulges beyond seven billion, these demands become greater. At the same time, climate change means a warmer planet, and many areas—including parts of North America—face serious drought conditions.

||||||
▼ IRRIGATION

Large-scale farming requires steady irrigation. Estimates put this use across the United States at **128 billion gallons** daily.

|||||||
▲ TEXTILE PRODUCTION

It takes **700 gallons** of water to sew, size, and dye every T-shirt manufactured in the United States.

||||||
◀ POWER GENERATION

Steam-driven turbine generators, which create thermoelectric power for households, use about **160 billion gallons** of water every day.

||||||
▲ HOUSEHOLD LEAKS

Every day, leaking pipes and faucets in U.S. household water systems lose at least **3 billion gallons**—literally down the drain.

||||||
▲ FRACKING

In eastern Pennsylvania alone, about **30 million gallons** of water are used daily to operate hydraulic fracturing wells—"fracking" operations—to extract natural gas.

||||||
▶ BOTTLED WATER

About **10 billion gallons** of water are bottled in the U.S. annually—that's about 150 bottles per person a year—and the number is growing rapidly.

"The United States leads the world in tornadoes, and we get these mondo hurricanes. We are [natural] disaster central. We've got everything but the frogs and the locusts, basically. We've got the fires, the floods—we've got all of that."

—DR. NEIL DEGRASSE TYSON

CHAPTER THREE

Where Do Storms Come From?

Tornadoes. Hurricanes. Floods. They're extreme-weather features—air, water, and heat mixing in different proportions to produce powerful releases of energy that can wreak havoc on our lives.

When it comes to storms, heat drives the bus. As the Sun shines, some parts of Earth (like the oceans) naturally absorb more light than others (like the polar ice caps). Temperature differences arise, and heat flows from warmer places to cooler ones. Storm fronts form where hot air and cold air collide. And if they happen to collide violently, right over your home, make sure your roof isn't leaking.

As with most things, storms aren't necessarily all bad. Hurricanes, for example, can bring lots of needed rainfall. Storms are just changes in the weather—until they get too severe. And the more heat there is to circulate and concentrate, the stronger a storm can get. We know Earth's surface is warming up. But by how much? Can—and should—we halt the heating? How much heat is too much? Hopefully, we won't have to find out the hard way.

Extreme-weather gear only goes so far.

Climate Confusion

What's the Difference Between Climate and Weather?

One classic way to understand climate is to think about the question of when you plant your tomatoes every spring. You plant by climate zone—an indicator that predicts the amount of rain they'll get in a given season, the typical date of the last frost, the average high summer temperature, the month when the leaves will change color, and so on. Those things are pretty predictable, year in and year out, based on climate.

Weather, on the other hand, is that late frost or heat wave or dry spell that forces you to take special care of your plants, or the sudden thunderstorm and lightning strike that knocks out electrical power to your house. These things change, hour to hour, day to day, and although the season when you're most likely to experience them might be regular, the day or night they happen is not.

"Weather is short-term, and climate is the average of weather over the longer term."

—ANDREW FREEDMAN, JOURNALIST

We like to think that climate is predictable—but climate changes, too. Indeed, ironically, some people deny the effects of global warming by saying, "Why worry? The climate's always changing!" Well, not so fast—literally.

And it does matter. Since the dawn of agriculture, every society that experienced a significant climate change was either dispersed or destroyed, and died out. If climate change happens to us, will we share the same fate? ■

BACK TO BASICS

What's the "Hockey Stick"?

Imagine a graph that starts rising slowly and then shoots upward: That's the "hockey stick." One dramatic version graphs the carbon dioxide level in Earth's atmosphere over time. For at least 400,000 years, the CO_2 level cycled between about 150 and 300 parts per million. Then in less than 0.02 percent of that time—just 70 years—the level shot up to 400 parts per million. The shape of the graph goes from a mostly horizontal line to a nearly vertical line almost instantaneously.

"Since 1880, there's been almost a degree Celsius warming . . . Up at the poles it's much, much more than that . . . on the order of three or four degrees Celsius . . . That's why you're seeing that melting . . . You get a positive feedback of warming."

—DR. CYNTHIA ROSENZWEIG, CLIMATOLOGIST

THINK ON THIS ▶ Is the Weather Getting Worse?

When the climate changes, weather changes, too—but it's only observable over long periods of time, and rarely with absolute certainty. By numerous measures, though, certain kinds of natural disasters have indeed become more common and more violent over the past several decades, especially those like droughts, floods, and hurricanes, which are driven by warmer air and water temperatures worldwide.

StarTalk Live!: Storms of Our Century (Part 1)

What Causes Severe Weather?

A lot of people seem to think the world is now experiencing more extreme weather events than ever. Astro-meteorologist Dr. Neil deGrasse Tyson wonders: "These intense storms . . . seem to be record-breaking in intensity and scale and size and damage . . . Where do these storms come from?"

Let's start by talking about any storm, extreme or not. Weather happens through the interaction of warm air, cold air, and water. Pockets of warm air rise upward, leaving a zone of low pressure below it; other air flows into that zone to equalize the pressure: That creates wind. The flow isn't always smooth and gentle, though—and if the warm air is moist, the water vapor in it will condense as it cools. That creates clouds and rain. Static electricity builds up in the clouds as they fly past one another, discharging in bolts of lightning. And if the process feeds back on itself and intensifies, you get thunderstorms, microbursts, tornadoes, and hurricanes.

To feed their severity, storms need energy—and that usually comes in the form of heat. Just in its water vapor alone, a typical weather system contains heat energy equivalent to numerous atomic bombs! ■

TOUR GUIDE

What Were the Worst Hurricanes in U.S. History?

1900: Galveston, Texas—an island eight feet above sea level—was wiped out by a storm surge 15 feet high. About 6,000 people died.

2005: Katrina, a Category 5 hurricane, pounded the U.S. Gulf Coast. In its wake, levees protecting New Orleans, Louisiana, were breached, flooding the city. More than 1,800 people died.

2012: Sandy became the largest "superstorm" in Atlantic history, its diameter stretching out more than 1,100 miles. It killed 233 people in eight countries and caused $75 billion worth of damage.

THINK ON THIS ▶ How Does the Hurricane Intensity Scale Work?

Hurricanes are classified by their maximum sustained wind speed. Category 1, at least 74 miles an hour; Category 2, at least 96; Category 3, at least 111; Category 4, at least 131; and Category 5, at least 156. "I once looked up the description of the damage at each one of these intensity scales," says Dr. Neil deGrasse Tyson, astro-inferno-cist. "It was like the descent into hell in a Dante story line . . . This is Earth trying to kill us."

> *"Earth has never had a stable crust. Just look around; it's churning daily. That's why we have earthquakes. Go look at the U.S. Geological Survey earthquake page on the Internet. It's a record of all the earthquakes in the world. There are like hundreds a day. Every day."*
>
> —DR. NEIL DEGRASSE TYSON, ASTRO-QUAKE-ICIST

Certain coasts are at higher risk for tsunamis.

What Causes Earthquakes, Volcanoes, and Tsunamis?

Earth's crust isn't a single solid piece—it's made of huge tectonic plates of rock, some of them millions of square miles in size. The plates slide around on Earth's mantle at the rate of a few inches per year—a barely noticeable rate. But when the plates run into each other, they can get stuck, and pressure builds.

That's the starting point for all these huge events. First come earthquakes—but we never quite know when. "Earthquakes actually are sourced in the mantle, that fluid portion below the brittle crust of our planet," explains volcanologist Dr. James Webster. "To actually be able to predict at any given moment in time what's going to happen in the immediate future becomes difficult."

In the end, if one plate buckles or slips, or the pressure otherwise suddenly releases, the earth quakes. If the pressure releases violently enough, the liquid rock below the plates belches upward onto the surface, and a volcano erupts. And if an undersea quake disturbs the water just wrong, a wall of water can surge outward from the quake's location, causing a tsunami, or tidal wave, and sweeping away everything in its path.

Thankfully, we've developed technology that enables us to predict natural disasters and measure their intensity. But it took time to make accurate systems. "The old Richter scale could not measure earthquakes that were of the highest magnitudes accurately," says planetary scientist Dr. Steven Soter. "So a new magnitude scale, based on what's called moment magnitude, was devised in the 1970s . . . It turns out to be a factor of 33 [times more powerful] for each magnitude . . . in terms of the amount of energy release." ∎

Smog clouds daylight in Nizhny Novgorod, Russia.

How Does the Greenhouse Effect Work?

DID YOU KNOW

On Earth, levels of greenhouse gases like carbon dioxide change naturally over many thousands of years. Humans, though, have managed to double the carbon dioxide level in less than two centuries—a hundred times faster than it would happen in nature without humanity's help.

Lying in bed on a cold night, your body heat radiates upward, cooling you down. If you have a blanket on, its fibrous layers will absorb some of the heat, creating a barrier of warmth so that your body loses heat more slowly and stays warmer. If you have a whole stack of blankets on, you'll retain even more heat and get nice and toasty.

That's how the greenhouse effect works. It's a misconception that carbon dioxide, methane, water vapor, or other greenhouse gas molecules reflect heat like glass. Rather, they absorb and reradiate infrared radiation—which we feel as heat—really well. They don't absorb visible light nearly as well, so sunlight can shine down on Earth's surface with no trouble. But terrestrial heat from any source—be it warming from the Sun, geothermal heat from Earth's interior, or humans burning fossil fuels—will leak upward and outward into space at a slower rate because of our blanket of greenhouse gases. ■

Revolving Around the Sun

What Effect Do Sunspots Have on Earth?

Sunspots are intense magnetic storms on the Sun's surface, many of them much larger than our entire planet. Although the total electromagnetic energy output increases where the sunspots are located, the temperature in those spots actually drops slightly, so they look dark compared to the solar background light. They don't make much of an impact on the heat and light we get from the Sun, but the resulting bursts of charged particles do make a difference here on Earth.

Dr. Judith Lean, a solar and atmospheric scientist, explains how these storms affect us: "The Sun controls the weather of the environment where satellites orbit and where radio waves communicate . . . If you want to connect with your iPhone, and a big solar storm comes along, smashes all that plasma into the Earth's magnetosphere, and affects the satellite that is connecting your communications, then you do care about the weather in space."

In the end, sunspots don't usually last more than a week or two, and the area of the Sun's surface they cover is small, so their total effect on Earth is usually tiny. ■

These black sunspots from 2013 measure more than six Earths across.

BACK TO BASICS

Are We Headed for Another Maunder Minimum?

The frequency of sunspots ebbs and flows, but every 11 years or so, the number reaches a peak—astronomers call that solar max. Then it dips down, reaches a minimum, and rises back up again. The most recent solar max was a dud, with barely half the number of spots compared to previous times. What's up with that? "This may be one of those unusually long cycles, or we may be going into something like the Maunder minimum, back in 1645, when sunspots disappeared for about 50 years," says Dr. Stephen Keil, solar scientist.

At the time of the Maunder minimum (named for two scientists, Annie and Walter Maunder, who first explained the period), temperatures worldwide also dropped slightly, the winters were longer than usual, and some historically ice-free rivers and lakes froze over. But that's not happening now—we're getting warmer.

DID YOU KNOW
Less than one percent of the Sun's surface is covered with sunspots. Other stars are known to have a surface more than 50 percent covered with spots.

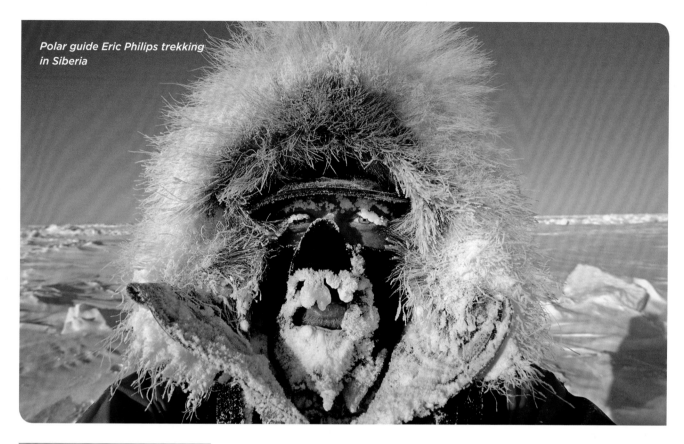

Polar guide Eric Philips trekking in Siberia

Is It Getting Cold Around Here?

"There are some places that are not as susceptible to natural disaster . . . What you want is to be in a place that is not as susceptible to the fluctuations in climate. And among those places would be rain forests, for example."

—DR. NEIL DEGRASSE TYSON, ASTRO-JUNGLE-IST

Serbian astrophysicist Milutin Milankovitch (1879–1958) made a number of detailed calculations that showed that tiny long-term variations in Earth's motion as it orbits the Sun can affect our climate in subtle yet important ways. The Milankovitch cycles have three main components: First, Earth precesses—that is, it wobbles like a top that's starting to fall—so the direction the North Pole points keeps changing. The Earth makes a full wobble once about every 23,000 years.

Second, there's the tilt angle of Earth's axis, which affects the lengths of the seasons and changes by about two degrees every 40,000 years. Third, the shape of Earth's orbit around the Sun changes, which affects the amount of sunlight Earth receives over the course of each year. It can change from slightly elliptical to nearly circular and back again about every 100,000 years.

Right now, Earth seems to be in the middle of the range of these cycles—so by Milankovitch's reckoning, our climate should be relatively moderate. ■

Climate Cycles:
Where's the Proof?

Earth's climate changes naturally, both locally and globally.
These changes happen over long periods of time, though,
whereas human-produced climate change has been rapid. What kinds
of evidence can we use to measure these changes and get the big picture?

|||||||
◀ OCEAN SEDIMENT

Fossilized plankton, diatoms, and other organisms buried deep beneath the ocean can show the environmental temperatures and conditions during which their bodies were built.

|||||||
▶ POLLEN

When these tiny grains are washed or blown into lakes and ponds, they get embedded in layers of sediment and provide a record of long-ago plant life—and the climate at the time that would support them.

|||||||
◀ ICE CORES

Tiny bubbles of air trapped in old, deep glaciers and packed ice preserve the greenhouse gas levels in Earth's atmosphere going back more than 500,000 years. We can track changes in those levels from then until now.

||||||
◀ ROCK

Wind-driven soil and sand deposits, such as loess and eolian dust, form during ice ages around the edges of massive glaciers. Layer by layer, they tell the history of some of Earth's most dramatic climate changes.

||||||
▲ CAVES

Mineral deposits formed from groundwater in underground caverns, like stalagmites and stalactites, record the climate in which they formed through the properties of their atoms and the thickness of their deposits.

||||||
▲ LAKE LEVELS

In drier parts of the world, the depths and areas of lakes can change dramatically when climate and moisture levels change. Fossil deposits along their shores trace that climate history.

||||||
▶ TREE RINGS

Paleoclimatologists can measure the environmental conditions and fire history of different parts of the world from the growth rings and fire scars of trees, as well as from charcoal in sediment records.

"The goal here really ought to be . . . a future where there's actually limitless energy, and we wouldn't even have to have these conversations, and we wouldn't have to be warming up the atmosphere, and having Earth do things that it hasn't done in a million years."

—DR. NEIL DEGRASSE TYSON, ASTRO-OPTIMIST

StarTalk Live!: Climate Change

Have We Reached the Tipping Point Yet?

Some research suggests there is a tipping point: a point at which, once Earth gets to a critical level of greenhouse gases or loses a certain amount of its polar ice, we will never be able to halt or reverse global warming. Is this possible? If so, are we there already?

Predicting the future accurately is always tough, even if you use the best tools available. And good scientists, like climatologist Cynthia Rosenzweig, readily acknowledge their limitations. "We use models, which are big mathematical sets of equations for the whole climate system . . . Are they doing a good job projecting? In general, they're doing a pretty good job, but some of these changes have been occurring faster than have been projected . . . Probably one of the most important examples is the melting of the polar ice caps."

Most climate change models in use today suggest that if a theoretical tipping point exists, we may be close to it, but we're not there yet. None of the models, though, can predict what scientific advances—or crazy natural events—will happen that could radically alter those predictions. ■

Human activities are pushing Earth to the edge.

TOUR GUIDE

How Is Agriculture Affecting Climate Change?

We tend to point to big industrial smokestacks and city traffic pollution as the causes for global warming and climate change, but what about the way we grow our food? "[Agriculture] itself is an emitter of greenhouse gases," says Cynthia Rosenzweig, a climatologist. "The livestock also, because of the enteric fermentation [the way cattle digest their food] puts a lot of methane out, which is a very powerful greenhouse gas . . . Creating nitrogen fertilizer is highly energy-intensive. Plus the fertilizer itself, when it's applied, emits another greenhouse gas: nitrous oxide."

So making food is contributing to global warming. And climate change is changing how we make food. Droughts are destroying the productivity of agricultural lands. Once-fertile coastal regions are now underwater or uninhabitable. And planting seasons are changing, affecting which crops can be grown. The list goes on.

"The mayors of cities around the world . . . have been getting together, and forming networks and signing on pacts with each other to set targets and timetables for greenhouse gas emissions."

—DR. CYNTHIA ROSENZWEIG, CLIMATOLOGIST

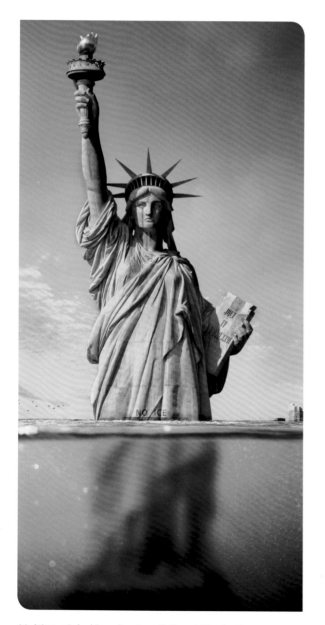

Melting global ice sheets will flood Manhattan.

Climate Confusion

How Can Climate Change Cause Both Droughts and Floods?

Extra heat is a versatile thing. Some hot places on Earth are deserts; others, tropical rain forests. When a hot place gets hotter, drought often results. And when a cold place heats up, its ice melts.

▶ HOW DOES MOISTURE RAMP UP CLIMATE CHANGE?

With ice melting and releasing liquid water, big climate change can occur. "When climate warms, even more moisture shows up, and then . . . it can rain heavier," says climatologist Dr. David Rind: "We've been seeing that for the last decade . . . heavier episodes of precipitation, more droughts, more floods, just an amplification."

▶ ARE THE SEAS ALREADY RISING?

You can ask the residents of South Florida, where ocean fish are washing up regularly on the streets of downtown Miami. Here's another data point, from climatologist Dr. Cynthia Rosenzweig: "These are the knock-on effects of warmer ocean temperatures . . . We have sea level rise, again, already happening. Just in New York City, we've had over the past 100 years, over a foot of sea level rise."

▶ DID CLIMATE CHANGE CAUSE SUPERSTORM SANDY?

No one storm can be linked directly to climate change, but the nature of a single storm can. "When any storm . . . comes along, the seas are [already] one foot higher, [so] the flooding goes one foot further in elevation," explains Dr. Rosenzweig. "So that extent of flooding that we had in Sandy, that is the actual direct link to climate change." ■

"I think the general attitude should be that we shouldn't waste the bounty of the Earth; that's the main thing."

—SIR DAVID ATTENBOROUGH, NATURALIST

CHAPTER FOUR

Is There a Solution for Pollution?

Plants and animals live, grow, and produce waste. In that sense, human pollution seems perfectly . . . natural. But just as industrialization has brought tremendous benefits to our species, the impacts of its waste extend far beyond mere inconvenience. Now our very existence seems to be threatened by the environmental changes we have wrought!

Happily, we are learning to clean up after ourselves. But as soon as we solve one dilemma, we have to tame a new monster. Until petroleum was first mined in the mid-1800s, we harvested oil from whales and they were being hunted nearly to extinction. Today we harvest fossil fuels from underground—and we have earthquakes caused by fracking. New York City streets were awash in horse manure until the advent of the automobile—and now we have smog and global warming.

What's our next step toward a healthy, pollution-free world? Is another solution coming? And what problems will come with it?

It is time to switch to renewable energy sources.

Were Prehistoric Sunsets Red?

Some people say that our red sunsets are caused by man-made particulates—that is, air pollution—scattering the light, more now than ever. So that raises the question: Would pre-pollution sunsets have been really boring? Not at all. To begin with, why does the sky look blue? It has to do with the atmosphere. If Earth didn't have an atmosphere, the sky would be black, even in the daytime. But we do have an atmosphere, full of air molecules, and as sunlight penetrates our atmosphere, those molecules

"It's not only pollution. It's pollen, it's water vapor, it's dust kicked up from deserts, it's volcanic particles—all those particles make a sunset red."

—DR. NEIL DEGRASSE TYSON, ASTRO-SUNSET-IST

scatter light in all directions. Turns out they scatter blue light much more effectively than red light, so it's mostly blue light that hits our eyes. As the Sun sets, its light is traveling through more air molecules to meet your eyes, and also past suspended particles that are larger than air molecules. The scattering of sunlight through the combined extra air and particulate matter make the sky at sunset look yellow, orange, and red. Any source of particles would do the trick. ∎

An illustration of Utahraptors running across a sunset-lit prehistoric grassland

The Story of Life on Earth With Sir David Attenborough

Can We Tax Our Way Out of Pollution?

In much of the world, carbon credits are a way of life. A government or business can get financial credit for steps taken to reduce CO_2 emissions and can use that credit to offset other carbon-producing processes they choose to continue. It's a way to keep CO_2 emissions at a lower level. Carbon credits have become an integral part of the economic and ecological dynamic in some countries. Could they come to the United States?

Bill Nye starts us down this road: "Oil companies, fossil fuel companies, already have this built in. They're anticipating a $40 per ton [of carbon dioxide emitted] surcharge that's in their economic modeling . . . If we did this, and then, the countries that don't produce as much carbon dioxide would have a tariff or a fee on the goods that were being imported that had a high carbon. This is not 'everything is going to be fine'; it is part of the solution." ∎

EXPERIENCE THE GRAVITY OF
HD 40307g A SUPER EARTH

BACK TO BASICS

If We Screw Earth Up, Can We Go to Another Planet?

As Neil tweeted, "Mysteries of #Interstellar: Can't imagine a future where escaping Earth via a wormhole is a better plan than just fixing Earth." From a purely scientific standpoint, it would take much, much less energy to repair our world than for all of us to travel to another one. Bill Nye chimes in: "This tradition of just, you've trashed an area, just move to a different area—just expand, just march on . . . We're going to have to be better stewards of the environment and, dare I say it, Neil, change the world."

DID YOU KNOW
Cooperation to reduce climate change among the major carbon-producing nations—China, the United States, the European Union, India, Russia, Indonesia, Brazil, Japan, Canada, and Mexico—could cover more than 70 percent of greenhouse gas emissions around the world.

THINK ON THIS ▶ Can GMOs Save Our Environment?

"The place to start is making . . . bacteria that could metabolize oil in an oil spill. That would be a really cool application . . . You could have some bacteria that could metabolize [the organic chemicals], and then leave behind all of the other stuff that comes out of oil wells—sulfur and so on—and let it sink to the bottom of the ocean." —Bill Nye the Science Guy

Can't We Just Plant More Trees?

Trees (and other plants) take in carbon dioxide and release oxygen. So if too much CO_2 is warming the globe, wouldn't more trees help? The Buddhist spiritual leader His Holiness the Gyalwang Drukpa, began a remarkable project a few years ago: Annually, thousands of volunteers gather with young saplings and plant trees in the Ladakh region of the Himalaya. In 2012 alone, they planted nearly 100,000 trees in a single hour!

The act of planting trees is simple, and when done wisely in a coordinated manner it can change an ecosystem for the better. Like any single action, of course, the effects of tree planting are limited, both ecologically and in time; the trees will take a long time to grow by human standards. And planting new trees may also have unintended consequences: Will they crowd out existing plant life by outcompeting them for resources? Would a large area covered with a single type of plant lead to increased disease and pest damage? Ultimately, though, events like these are a great way to start a good thing. ∎

More trees won't be the only answer.

BACK TO BASICS

Bill Nye's Words of Wisdom About Climate Change

"It's going to be a close call. It's not clear who is going to get to the buoy first: the climate change that undoes so many of our urban populations and causes enormous upheaval, or the scientifically literate populace that is emerging with an enthusiasm for scientific truth, and understanding the world by critical thinking . . . And so when I say it's a close call, I mean: We could lose. Humankind could really be in huge trouble. Not just the coastal populations in the developing world, but everybody could be in trouble. So this is why . . . it's a race. This is why we do what we do."
—Bill Nye the Close Call Guy

"When you pump large amounts of water underground, you loosen up some of those faults, and they move, and you've got earthquakes. Fortunately, the earthquakes you get from [fracking] tend to be shallow, and rather small. And there's even the argument that that's good, because they're relieving tension on the faults, which otherwise would build up and eventually result in a larger earthquake . . . It does speak to the fact that there are unintended consequences when we start . . . altering the Earth in intense ways."
—DR. DAVID GRINSPOON,
ASTROBIOLOGIST, ON IF FRACKING CAUSES EARTHQUAKES

Can We Afford Electric Cars and Solar Panels?

Going all-electric would be great. It costs a lot to retool for the future, though. Dr. Neil deGrasse Tyson, astro-budget-ist, asks: "So, do you have a plan? What's your plan? Because as long as oil is cheap and it's cheaper than my solar panels, how do you expect people to [afford it] . . . If you're rich, you can buy the car that saves gas, that costs you more than the car that doesn't save gas."

Neil posed the problem to his friend Bill Nye the Science Guy: How can we possibly afford electric cars and solar panels?

Bill Nye replied: "To maintain our current way of life, can we afford *not* to have them?"

People complain about emission standards and other such rules. "The big thing as we say about climate change, is: If you are opposed to government regulation now, you don't like governments now, just wait till stuff gets bad," Nye says. "Just wait till Floridians have to abandon their homes and Miami is half underwater—and then there's going to be regulation." ∎

An electric car with a photovoltaic roof

BACK TO BASICS

How Will We Solve Energy Storage?

To compete with fossil fuels, solar- and wind-power generation needs to be consistent, reliable, and controllable. But skies get cloudy and winds stop blowing—and not always when you expect it. And electric cars can only go so far, because they can't store enough energy between charges.

Both of these problems can be solved with rechargeable batteries that are small and light, and hold a lot of charge. But we're definitely not there yet. Current electric vehicles have a range of about one mile for every four to eight pounds of batteries in the car, and big power stations have to be able to hold and distribute much more power at any one time than a warehouse full of such batteries could manage.

Optimistic projections suggest that at least one new battery technology, the lithium-air battery, could replace the current lithium-ion battery in about 10 years. That would result in an 80 percent weight reduction. A lot can happen in 10 years, though.

Reporting on Science (Part 2)

Is the Climate-Change Debate Fair and Balanced?

Journalists believe in giving both sides of a story. In science, rival hypotheses are considered, too—until a clear consensus emerges due to overwhelming evidence. Science correspondent Miles O'Brien describes where we are on the topic of climate change: "Some stories have one side that is represented by, say, 95 percent of the scientific community in the world. Is it fair, in a story about climate change, which I'm obviously talking about, to do this classic journalistic convention of 'equal time for both sides'? . . . Is that serving the truth? I would submit to you, not. As a matter of fact, that is feeding obfuscation; that is actually perpetuating a myth—dare I say, a lie . . . The scientific jury is in, here."

On the subject of climate change, the data clearly show that Earth is warming up, and that humans are contributing to the warming. That's the fairest assessment of the evidence. ■

> *"There is no more scientific debate. There's a political debate; there's a debate over money —over how we should spend it, what we should do. But there is no scientific debate. Let's just get over that."*
>
> **—MILES O'BRIEN,**
> PBS SCIENCE CORRESPONDENT

BIOGRAPHY
👓

Why Should the Pope Address Climate Change?

Pope Francis, born Jorge Mario Bergoglio in Buenos Aires, Argentina, worked as a chemical technician before joining the priesthood. When the Pope speaks of climate change and its harmful effects on the poor people of the world, some are skeptical of a religious leader interested in science. Others applaud him. "Reason and faith are not inconsistent. Logic and faith are not inconsistent," says Rev. James Martin of the Society of Jesus. "Pope Francis, who starts with faith—he's naturally interested in the natural world. He wants to know more about God's creation, and so why not study chemistry?"

THINK ON THIS ▶ Could Magma Clean up the Pacific Garbage?

"That's the kind of creative thinking that we really need. How do you really get rid of plastic? Sure, put it in a subduction zone and send it to the mantle of the Earth. I'm all for it, if I could see the details . . . There's nothing that sounds wacky about it to me."
—Dr. David Grinspoon, astrobiologist

Is the Solution to Stop Burning Fossil Fuels?

Some say we should banish fossil fuels from our future. "[They say] we have come to demonize the consumption of energy . . . That's the wrong attitude, in my opinion," says astro-energy-ist Dr. Neil deGrasse Tyson. "If you're going to demonize something, demonize that which alters your environment. The universe has limitless energy . . . I'd be embarrassed to tell an alien, who just moved through the vacuum of space bathed in limitless starlight, that here on Earth we kill one another to extract oil . . . Is the solution to stop burning fossil fuels, or is there some other solution that comes along, that doesn't negate this, it just renders it completely obsolete, as the car did to the horse?"

▶ WHAT GOOD CAN COME FROM BURNING OIL?

Actually, a whole lot of good comes from burning oil. Among other things, oil keeps us warm in the winter and cool in the summer, it gets us to places near and far through various means of transportation, and it allows us to be productive and contribute to the local and global economy. The problem is in the medium term and long term—a couple of human generations or more from now—when the environmental consequences of burning that oil threaten to undo all of that short-term benefit.

▶ WHY DON'T WE JUST INNOVATE OUR WAY OUT OF USING OIL?

Plenty of people are working toward that very goal. Including entrepreneur Elon Musk, founder of Tesla Motors and SpaceX: "If we don't find a solution to burning oil for transport and we then run out of oil, the economy will collapse and civilization will come to an end as we know it . . . We have to ultimately get off oil no matter what." ■

"Why would you run this crazy experiment of changing the chemical composition of the atmosphere and oceans by adding enormous amounts of carbon dioxide that have been buried since the Precambrian era? That's crazy. That is the dumbest experiment in history by far."

—ELON MUSK, FOUNDER OF TESLA MOTORS AND SPACEX

"You read about the Mayan calendar, you've heard about the Apocalypse, and your brain just connects the dots—and then you become certain that the world will end."

—DR. NEIL DEGRASSE TYSON, APOCALYPS-ICIST

CHAPTER FIVE

Is This the End of the World as We Know It?

Armageddon. Ragnarok. The "end of days." Why, in the annals of superstition, myth, and prophecy, is humanity's collective demise such a popular theme? Psychologists who study apocalyptic impulses say that if we've all gotta go sometime, most of us would rather all go down together, in a blaze of glory, than alone, unnoticed, and forgotten.

In early cultures, it was natural disasters that destroyed everything. As we started understanding the forces of nature, people turned to the supernatural, like the devil, who was supposed to be let loose upon the world in the year 1000. Today, religious motifs are being replaced by pseudoscience—people mixing parts of scientific concepts and plausible-sounding statements to create fictional scenarios that only slightly resemble reality.

Yes, we face real dangers, for which we can study and prepare. How can we tell the difference between fact and flimflam? Armed with scientific literacy, we can look to the future unafraid.

Are we looking at an apocalypse
on planet Earth?

The End Is Nigh—or Is It?

When hysteria broke out surrounding the Mayan predicted 2012 apocalypse, Neil took to Twitter to clear things up. "End-of-world prophecies for 2012 are hoaxes perpetrated by the scientific illterate on the scientifically under informed." There have been many renditions about the end of the world—from the Sun burning out to asteroids hitting Earth. So far none have come to fruition. Here's a list of recent—and yes, wrong—apocalyptic predictions.

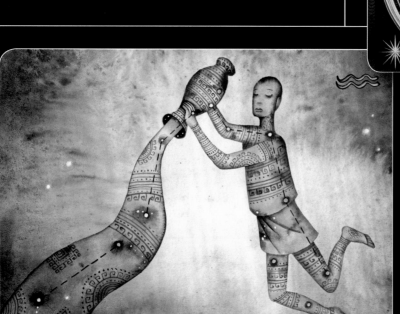

||||||
◀ 1962 PLANETARY ALIGNMENT

A planetary alignment coincided with an Earth-Moon perigee, and high winds created storms and high tides in the eastern United States. Despite disclaimers from meteorologists, many people extrapolated flood warnings to mean global doom.

||||||
▶ 1997 HEAVEN'S GATE

The beautiful passage of comet Hale-Bopp led to the tragic group suicide of 39 members of the Heaven's Gate cult, who believed they would be transported to a spaceship hiding in the comet's tail.

◀ 2000 Y2K

Computers unable to handle the year change from 1999 to 2000 were expected to fail and predicted to lead to catastrophes everywhere from banks to airports to nuclear power plants. Millions of dollars were spent on "Y2K" upgrades. Ultimately, 1/1/00 came and went.

Comet Elenin

||||||

▲ 2011 COMET ELENIN

As comet Elenin approached, some claimed it was actually a rogue planet named Nibiru, whose arrival would cause planetary destruction. The comet broke into pieces before ever reaching Earth.

|||||

2012 MAYAN CALENDAR

n ancient Mayan calendar agment was said to tell of e end to a "cosmic cycle" n December 21, 2012. wide variety of ways in hich the world would nd on that date circulated. one of them happened.

What Would Abe Lincoln Do?

There's an interesting story about Abe Lincoln and his response to a Leonid meteor storm that occurred in 1833. Neil tells the tale: "The local preacher was well-read in the Bible, of course, where in the Book of Revelation it says at the end of days, stars will fall from the sky and land on Earth. So he sees this, he comes running, knocking on doors, goes into Abe's room, and says, 'The end of the world is near. Repent.' Lincoln comes running out. He looks up, sees this beautiful meteor shower, but also notices that all the stars that he's familiar with are still there. The Big Dipper. Orion. So he goes back in and goes back to sleep . . . It helps to know a little astrophysics. He was well read—better read, apparently, than the preacher." ■

||

015 BLOOD MOON PHECY

Christian ministers claimed the "blood moon prophecy" the Book of Revelation, ling the end-time, would e to pass during the lunar se of September 27–28, . It didn't.

Cosmic Queries: Planet Earth

Can We Survive a Magnetic Polar Reversal?

DID YOU KNOW
A medical MRI scanner has a magnetic field strength 100,000 times stronger than Earth's magnetic field at our planet's surface. The world's most powerful magnets are another 100 times stronger than that.

Magnetic fields, like magnets, have north and south poles. Over long periods of time, magnetic fields can switch their polarity—north becomes south, south becomes north. The Sun does this once every 11 years—and based on the fossil record, Earth appears to have done it hundreds of times in the past, most recently about 800,000 years ago.

> "You can look at the fossil record. Last time around, while we had zero magnetic field, they carried on making babies just fine. So it does not appear to be as severe as you might think, the evidence shows."
> —DR. NEIL DEGRASSE TYSON

Recently, after scientific satellites measured Earth's magnetic field to have changed slightly, doomsayers began to claim that a magnetic polar reversal was on its way—and at the moment of the flip, we'd lose our magnetic protection from solar wind, and life on Earth would be wiped out.

Is this likely? No. Just because the poles reverse doesn't mean the magnetic field goes away—it just changes orientation, and it happens gradually and erratically. Even if a short dip or switch in field strength were to occur for any reason, we'd still have enough protection from Earth's atmosphere to weather the solar wind. It's just a natural phenomenon—a neat feature of our planet, not a problem. ■

Earth's magnetic field is more complex than a horseshoe magnet.

DID YOU KNOW
The Andromeda galaxy is on a collision course with the Milky Way! Don't worry, though—it won't happen for at least four billion years, and even then the Sun isn't likely to take a direct hit from another star.

On the Scale of the Universe, Does Size Really Matter?

"In the year 1900 if you asked people what they were most worried about, it was overpopulation, and lack of food, and all this. They were not worried about asteroids. In a century, what will people be listing as the biggest risk to their lives? We have no idea. That's why it's good to learn what's out there."

—DR. NEIL DEGRASSE TYSON

When it comes to objects hitting Earth, you better believe size matters. A lot of stuff is continuously striking our planet, and we barely notice any of it, thanks to their small size. "Earth plows through several hundred tons of meteors a day. Some of that stuff falls in the day-time—you don't see it because it was bright," Neil explains. "And then, at night, are you looking up? Was it cloudy? Was it overcast? So you don't catch all of it when it falls. Most of it burns up, as what we call a meteor streak. But some of it is big enough to land—and then the meteor becomes a meteorite."

"Apophis is my favorite asteroid out there. It's the asteroid that's the size of the Rose Bowl that's headed our way. And it's not *going to hit us on April 13, 2029 (which, by the way, is a Friday, in case you were wondering)."*

—DR. NEIL DEGRASSE TYSON

So, yes, in this case size really, really matters. If a single object the size of an apartment building were to hit us, it could flatten a whole city. But if that object were a mile across, all of human civilization would be at risk. ∎

THINK ON THIS ▶ Can We Just Send Bruce Willis?

In the movie *Armageddon* oil-workers-turned-astronauts zoom out to direct an asteroid away from Earth with a huge nuclear blast. Is there any reality to that?

DR. AMY MAINZER: If you have enough time, you might be able to do something that's just a simple kinetic impactor.

CHUCK NICE: Just like your health, early detection is the key.

Will the Universe End in Fire or Ice?

"Some say the world will end in fire, / Some say in ice." Poet Robert Frost was talking metaphorically about love and hate—but we can certainly get astrophysical and apply his words to the end of the universe, too. "Take the temperature of the universe—they call it the cosmic microwave background," explains astro-lights-out-ist Dr. Neil deGrasse Tyson. "You can actually stick a thermometer in it and get a reading. It's about three degrees above absolute zero, and we're about 14 billion years old. When we're 28 billion years old, we'll be about one and a half degrees, and it'll scale right on down until we asymptotically approach zero.

> *"When you move metals you can end up generating currents, and if you have a current, you also have a magnetic field."*
>
> **–DR. NEIL DEGRASSE TYSON, ASTRO-MAGNET-ICIST**

"The temperature of the universe will continue to get cooler and cooler and cooler. Stars will eventually run out of their fuel. They will die. Then all matter will be left in the remnants, the dead cold remnants of stars. Once these energy sources run out, the stars will turn off one by one, the galaxies will shut off, and the universe will turn dark for the remainder of eternity."

So that's it, lights out? At least we're billions of years away from utter darkness. ■

TOUR GUIDE

What's First: the Expansion of the Sun or the Loss of Our Magnetic Field?

Earth's magnetic field strength could drop drastically if internal motions, called convection currents, stopped in Earth's iron-nickel core. Current research suggests they might—a giant meteor impact could do it—but they would eventually resume.

Meanwhile, we know that the Sun will transform into a red giant and engulf our planet in about five billion years. So which comes first? "We'll probably lose our dynamo before the death of the Earth," says Neil. "'Dynamo' is lingo for the movement of molten iron."

Answer, an educated guess: The magnetic field goes first.

THINK ON THIS ▶ Can We Stop the Sun From Burning Out?

Nope. The Sun produces more energy in a thousandth of a second than the total of all the energy ever generated by humans in the history of civilization. Astrophysically speaking, it's possible to keep nuclear fusion in a star going by adding mass to it—perhaps when another star falls into it and merges with it. When we humans can make that happen, we'll be so advanced we won't need the Sun to survive anyway.

Can We Avoid the Fate of the Dinosaurs?

D r. Hubbard knows what he's talking about. He's run NASA's Mars program, founded the NASA Astrobiology Institute, and is the architect of the Sentinel mission to detect killer asteroids. He's not insulting the dinosaurs, mind you: They dominated Earth for more than 150 million years. (We humans haven't even been here 5 million.) Then, 65 million years ago, a meteor 10 miles wide crashed into Earth's surface. It was the evolutionary blow that sealed their fate.

Dinosaurs hadn't evolved far enough to build tools and machinery. But humans have, and so today we can at least find killer meteors before they hit us. If we find one, what can we do?

"The reason that dinosaurs went extinct is because they didn't have a space program."

—DR. G. SCOTT HUBBARD, ASTRONAUTICIST AND AERONAUTICIST

Astrophysicist Dr. Amy Mainzer says we could smack it. "There are options to deflect it simply by whacking into it. Just hit it. The Deep Impact mission actually did that with a comet in 2005—just ran into the comet. And that actually can push something, if you have enough time."

Or we could paint it. You read that right. Neil shows us his artistic side and tells us how: "Because asteroids are dark, if you paint it white, it will reflect sunlight, and the sunlight bouncing off of that side will serve as a kind of mild propulsion to push it out of harm's way. But the problem is, it's not a big push; it's a gentle push." ∎

Asteroids rain down on the last days of the dinosaurs.

Time Travel at the Movies

What Happens When a Nuclear Bomb Detonates?

At least one doomsday scenario is real: If a significant fraction of the 20,000 or so nuclear bombs in the world's arsenals were detonated, the energy released would approach that of a one-mile-wide asteroid striking Earth. Until the 1990s, when the Cold War ended, people lay awake at night worrying about such a scenario. We may not worry as much today, but the possibility is still out there, and real.

> "You get the air, the expanding air, which then blows everything into the winds. All we are is dust in the wind."
>
> —DR. NEIL DEGRASSE TYSON

Nuclear warheads harness the power of fission, as large atoms like uranium and plutonium are broken apart, or fusion, as small atoms like hydrogen are combined. These processes convert matter into energy, which comes out as light in many wavelengths—from gamma rays to radio waves—and kinetic energy, in the form of shock waves and winds. Fission and fusion also produce vast amounts of radioactive by-products that can survive for years, even centuries, after a nuclear warhead has been detonated. These by-products can create long-lasting health hazards. ■

An atomic explosion and shock wave

LAUGH OUT LOUD ▶ With Neil and Chuck Nice, Comedian

NEIL: I'm more afraid of zombies than dinosaurs. The big dinosaurs with the big teeth—they did not survive the asteroid.

CHUCK: So they are living underground. They're just oil now.

NEIL: Soon to exact their revenge on our ecosystem by increasing our carbon footprint. The revenge of the dinosaurs. Actually, our oil is mostly vegetation.

The Future of Humanity With Elon Musk

Should We Be Afraid of Artificial Intelligence?

Opinions differ widely about the benefits or dangers of artificially created sentience, from Wall-E to Skynet. Here are two divergent views, from Elon Musk, founder of Tesla Motors and SpaceX, and Bill Nye the AI Guy:

"I'm quite worried about artificial superintelligence these days," says Musk. "I think it's . . . maybe something more dangerous than nuclear weapons . . . What does it try to optimize? And we need to be really careful with saying, 'Oh, how about human happiness?' Because it may conclude that all unhappy humans should be terminated, or that we should all just be captured and [have] dopamine and serotonin directly injected into our brains . . . We should exercise caution."

Nye is more optimistic: "I'm all for the singularity when computers are as smart as people. But computers, and the quantum-computing thing, run on electricity . . . The robots show up in western China and there's no place to plug in . . . They're not very productive, let alone take-over-the-world-ive. There's a lot of other things to worry about."

Artificially intelligent beings will probably wind up exactly like natural intelligent beings. Which ones will be more dangerous? ■

Designing AI requires that we define human intelligence and emotion.

TOUR GUIDE

Is IBM's Watson Intelligent?

Watson was programmed to be a contestant on the quiz show *Jeopardy!*—and soundly defeated its human competition. "I would call [Watson] intelligent, but I wouldn't call it 'near-human,'" says Stephen Gorevan, chairman of Honeybee Robotics. "There are degrees of accumulated knowledge and organized ability, and I think that when you get . . . into the realm of art, you'd see the difference."

Who defines intelligence, anyway? Neil and Stephen are both knowledgeable and intelligent, after all—and Watson could beat either of them at *Jeopardy!* Maybe Watson wouldn't call them "near-Watson."

"If there was a very deep digital superintelligence that was created that could go into rapid recursive self-improvement in a nonlogarithmic way, then . . . it could reprogram itself to be smarter and iterate very quickly, and do that 24 hours a day on millions of computers. Well . . . that's all she wrote . . . We would be like a pet Labrador—if we're lucky."
—ELON MUSK, FOUNDER OF TESLA MOTORS AND SPACEX

Who's More Dangerous: Humans or Cyanobacteria?

Cyanobacteria—also known as blue-green algae—were the first Earth organisms to use photosynthesis, which combines carbon dioxide and water to make sugar compounds for food. "The cyanobacteria, 2.2 billion years ago, evolved photosynthesis, and they thought, 'Here's a great energy source, sunlight; this is wonderful,'" explains astrobiologist Dr. David Grinspoon. "And they started polluting the air with oxygen, which caused a catastrophe and wiped out most of the species that were alive then."

"So interestingly, we're not the first species to come along and, in the quest for an energy source, screw up the planet."

—DR. DAVID GRINSPOON, ASTROBIOLOGIST

Thanks to the presence of cyanobacteria, oxygen gas—the waste product of photosynthesis—eventually supplanted carbon dioxide in Earth's atmosphere. It took a long time for primitive life on Earth to evolve to use that oxygen, which is still deadly to a lot of modern-day microbes. But it also took the cyanobacteria a very long time to poison the air.

Compare the effects of cyanobacteria with the climate change we are seeing today—rapid changes to the Earth's atmosphere from greenhouse gases. For better or worse, we humans seem to be doing in just a few centuries what it took cyanobacteria eons to achieve. ■

Microorganisms find strength in numbers.

DID YOU KNOW

There are an estimated 2,000 to 8,000 species of cyanobacteria, and they can survive in almost every kind of ecosystem on Earth.

LAUGH OUT LOUD ▶ **With Michael Che, Comedian**

"I heard that the cows fart and it's ruining everything, but it seems like a hilarious way to go . . . What if it was written in . . . like an ancient book, that someday the cows will all fart at the same time, and that will be the end of mankind? . . . But it's stranger than fiction."

Cosmic Queries: Mayan Apocalypse and Other Disasters

Could a Doomsday Solar Flare Wipe Out Life on Earth?

Solar flares regularly burst forth from the Sun and spray radiation and solar particles into the solar system. A solar flare is unlikely to cause our extinction, but it might be strong enough to create a serious electrical headache. "If this flare is particularly potent, charged particles can reach lower in our atmosphere and affect our communications satellites," says Neil. "Our satellites run on electrical currents. If you have charged particles swarming electrical devices, you can create short circuits. A really big flare could sort of leave us . . . communications-blind. And the electrical grid could also be affected, because if a flare gets really low it can reach the Earth and short-circuit it. We've got top people working on it, but we are susceptible." ∎

"If the global climate changes in ways that our systems cannot respond to, it would mean widespread death, given how we now are dependent on the equilibrium and stability of the system that we created for ourselves."
—DR. NEIL DEGRASSE TYSON

Solar flares can extend thousands of miles above the Sun's surface.

BACK TO BASICS

Are You Scientifically Literate?

Science literacy, if you have it, can act like a sixth sense—an intuitive feeling that tells you if what you're seeing and hearing is plausible or ridiculous. "Science literacy is not what you know. It's how is your brain is wired for asking questions," says Neil. "When you study how the actual universe works, you're in a position to then inoculate yourself against the charlatans out there who would have you believe the world would end, and as a result, have you join their cult or hand them money."

The great news is that science literacy isn't a supernatural gift. Everyone can learn it. First, get a sense of numbers—how big, how small, how many, and how much. Then, get a sense of how numbers and facts can be organized into useful information—how data should and shouldn't be interpreted. Finally, get a sense of how data can be gathered and combined to confirm or refute ideas. Never be afraid to ask questions. If you're scientifically literate and your gut tells you to be skeptical, then you're more than likely correct.

BEING HUMAN

We build. We create. We've walked on the Moon. We've constructed communities and vast cities and great monuments. We laugh, sing, play, eat, drink, and love. Being human is awesome! We also demolish. We destroy. We've wiped out ecosystems. We've waged wars, leveled cities, and committed terrible violence. We cry, scream, fight, puke, choke, and hate. Being human is scary! How did humanity get this way? How will we change in the future? Those questions have answers only if a human being can know the meaning of being human.

*"The truffle is $1,500. The peach is $1.
Which is better? The truffle is rarer,
it costs more money, but is it more delicious than
a perfectly ripe peach in season? Or a pear?"*

—ANTHONY BOURDAIN, CHEF AND TV HOST

CHAPTER ONE

What's the Spice of Life?

Food! Glorious food! Thousands of years of growing, raising, and cooking food have created a legacy of deliciousness. The typical spice cabinet has dozens of flavorings, a typical kitchen a hundred ingredients. With practice, we all can make whatever we want to eat, exactly when we want it.

Indeed, we have gone past producing the optimal amount of food available for all, vaulted over the point of excess, and then kept going. For almost the entire history of humanity, the acquisition of nutrition has been a life-or-death struggle. Today, more and more of us have so much food that we're actually suffering the health consequences. In part, it's our ancient cravings for sugar, salt, and fat, combined with science funded by business interests. Happily, there's plenty we can do to fend off the bad effects of this gluttony in our daily lives while still eating well at home and as we travel.

So eat, drink, and be merry! Not too much, though—for tomorrow, we shall dine again.

Everything You Need to Know About Salt

Ancient Roman soldiers were paid with salt—hence the term "salary."
ven though it's cheap today, salt has tremendous power. Its food-preservi
d taste-enhancing properties have shaped our society—and our bodies, to

||||||||

◀ WHAT MAKES GOURMET SALT COLORFUL?

"Until modern times, a goal of salt producers was to try to get all that stuff out and try to get it as white as possible . . . Every color is an impurity." —Mark Kurlansky, author of *Salt: A World History*

||||||||

▶ HOW MANY USES OF SALT ARE THERE?

"The U.S. is the largest producer and consumer of salt in the world . . . And guess what—only 8 percent of that is used for food . . . The industry claims 14,000 uses for salt." —Dr. Neil deGrasse Tyson, astro-salt-icist

||||||

▲ CAN SALT REALLY
KILL YOU?

Ingesting too much salt at once can cause
seizures and death. That's a rare concern,
though—you would have to eat several cups
for that to happen. A little too much salt each
day—say, 0.03 ounce, or about 1,000 milli-
grams—is the more insidious danger.

||||||

▲ HOW DOES NEIL KEEP
HIS BROCCOLI SO GREEN?

"Put in a dash of salt while you're boiling
vegetables and it keeps the color of your
broccoli bright and green, rather than that
faded green you get in canned vegetables."
—Dr. Neil deGrasse Tyson, astro-broccol-ist

FOOD FOR THOUGHT
Are You Worth Your Salt?

The ancient consideration of salt as a high-value commodity shows
through in our language today, including in the phrase "to be worth your
salt." "Basically the entire food trade depended on salt," says Mark Kurlansky, author of *Salt: A World History*. "And in preindustrial society, that
was a very large part of trade. So it's not an exaggeration to say that
without salt, you couldn't have an international economy."

And it isn't just in western European history that salt has a value going
back centuries. "In the southwestern pueblos, it was very much of a commodity that people traded back and forth, and that goes back 3,000 to
4,000 years . . . Hopis still have a salt pilgrimage that they go on . . . to this day," says anthropologist
Dr. Peter Whiteley. ■

Are Yummy and Yuck Acquired Tastes?

Chef and TV host Anthony Bourdain shares how he enjoys the variety of global cuisine: "I got over using words like 'bizarre' a long time ago when looking at how other people eat around the world. There are whole spectrums of flavors that other countries, other cultures, take for granted and require in their diet. In the Philippines, there's a whole bitter component that we are almost instinctively not happy with. They will introduce bile into dishes to give it that welcome bitter note.

"In cultures like Scandinavian cultures, where there's a very limited spectrum of flavors—not a lot of spices traditionally, a lot of fresh fish, fresh fish, frozen fish, more fresh fish, maybe some preserved fish—as well as South Pacific cultures, where it's all sort of sweet fresh fish, not a lot of salty, savory, there's a tradition of rotting things, like fermenting fish, getting it really offensively funky by our standards, just 'cause, I think, out of boredom. And it's worth noting also that we, Western societies, anyway, used to do that. In Roman times, the condiment of choice was something called garam, that was essentially rotten fish guts, and rotten fish sauce; this was the salt, the principal seasoning ingredient all across Europe. So even our own tastes have changed." ■

U.K. consumers tasted oddball flavors of Walkers chips and voted for their favorite.

THINK ON THIS ▶ Can Candy Make You Smarter?

DR. MAYIM BIALIK: The issue there is motivation, and not necessarily a skill set and a cognitive ability or a technical ability. The fact is, yes, candy makes everything better, no matter what you're trying to learn, because it's a very strong motivator.

DR. HEATHER BERLIN: It might not make you better at math, but it might make you study for longer.

Too Little or Too Much?

Billions of people worldwide don't get enough to eat, and yet Americans are still getting fat. And much of the rest of the world, alas, is trending our way. "What's happening in the developing countries now is that as everybody gets a little money, they start eating more, and they start eating like we do, and they put on weight and develop type 2 diabetes, and there it goes," says Dr. Marion Nestle, author of *Food Politics*. "It even has a name. It's called the 'nutrition transition.'"

▸ HOW DO I KNOW WHEN TO STOP?

"We have about a hundred physiological factors that encourage us to eat more," explains Dr. Nestle. "We're not very well tuned to the environment that we're in, and our physiology is much better at saying, 'Eat, eat, eat, eat. You're hungry—better get the glucose to the brain quick,' and much, much less effective at telling us when to stop."

▸ WHY ARE VEGANS BETTER OFF IN NONINDUSTRIALIZED COUNTRIES?

"One of my favorite statistics is that apparently vegans in nonindustrialized cultures seem to do much better than vegans in industrialized cultures," says chef and TV host Anthony Bourdain. "Apparently, the insect parts and carcasses in rice are much higher in nonindustrialized cultures, so basically they're getting a lot more animal protein. They're very high in protein—bugs—by the way."

▸ HOW MUCH DOES OBESITY COST THE U.S.?

Dr. Nestle offers one figure: "There have been estimates—I don't know how good they are—that overweight costs America $190 billion a year."

"You can go to Mars twice for that," adds Neil. ∎

Is the Food Industry Killing Us?

Since time immemorial, people have sold stuff to other people, whether or not it's beneficial or necessary. You see it every day in the supermarket aisles, says chef and TV host Anthony Bourdain: "With the good comes the bad, and the bad might be that it is in the financial interest of some very large, powerful companies that you continue to eat badly, and too much. And they're going to continue to spend a lot of money, as any company will do, to make you continue to buy their products. And a lot of these products are not ideal staples of any diet."

Sometimes the public gets a glimpse of what's really going on. Consider the recent dustup over "pink slime." Bourdain explains: "Pink slime is not an ingredient, according to the rules. It is a process that allowed ground-beef manufacturers to essentially buy the outer cuts of beef that would otherwise previously have had to be discarded . . . [because they can] contain *E. coli* . . . By introducing, as I understand it, an ammonia vapor—basically steaming this stuff—and whipping it into a mulch-like paste with bits of extruded fat—mixing it into this slime and processing it with ammonia—they were able to bring the likelihood of *E. coli* down." ■

The notorious "pink slime" beef

BACK TO BASICS

What Is the Essence of a Peach?

In the secret vaults of food-company laboratories, scientists have for years sought to isolate and re-create the tastes, smells, and textures of the foods we know. Artificial food products like Velveeta, Jell-O, and Tang permeate modern food culture. What about the highbrow version of this edible engineering—the molecular food movement?

"It's treating ingredients in new ways," says chef and TV host Anthony Bourdain. "It's manipulating preexisting ingredients into unusual forms . . . to trick the mind into eating a strawberry that doesn't look like a strawberry, an apple that looks and feels like caviar in the mouth . . . It's not chemistry class, but it certainly does look like a laboratory."

"The fact that McDonald's and other retail outlets are saying, 'We're not using it anymore'—it's not like they're nice guys. They're looking pretty far into the future and seeing, 'This is going to come back and bite us.' "

—ANTHONY BOURDAIN, CHEF AND TV HOST, ON RESTAURANTS' USE OF "PINK SLIME"

How Do I Avoid Getting Sick While Traveling?

It's tempting to try every possible exotic food when you're traveling. Street food vendors are often nearly irresistible. In almost every case, though, you'll be better off eating properly washed and fully cooked things. Even if that may kill the buzz in trying the most enticing local delicacies, you'll generally be healthier if you kill the harmful microbes in your food.

Here's some more stomach-saving advice from globe-hopping chef Anthony Bourdain, who's been around the block enough times to know from experience what not to do:

> **1.** "Exercising reasonable caution, the same way you would if you travel around rural America, is a useful thing to do wherever you go."

> **2.** "Always ask yourself, is this how your average person eats. Is the place busy?"

> **3.** "If you're aware that avian flu has become a concern in the area, undercooked poultry is probably not going to be a good idea . . . You have to think about those things. If there's mad cow [disease] in the area, maybe calf's brains at a dodgy pub would not be your first option."

> **4.** "Just common sense. If they're not drinking the water in Russia from the tap, maybe you shouldn't either." ∎

> "Cooking does wonders for food safety . . . You will be so much better off eating cooked food in places where the water's dirty."
> —DR. MARION NESTLE, AUTHOR OF *FOOD POLITICS*

Chef and TV host Anthony Bourdain has put his stomach to the test.

> *"I think [people eat blowfish sushi] because of the risk of dying . . . Tetrodotoxin is the poison . . . What's amazing is that it does not affect your heart, so you get to stay alive while you're dying."*
> —DR. MARK SIDDALL, BIOLOGIST

THINK ON THIS ▶ Is Drinking Blood From a Beating Cobra Heart Safe?

A cobra's blood has no venom in it, as long as you stay clear of the fangs, but that doesn't mean it's safe to consume. That's why we couldn't believe Anthony Bourdain had tried it! "[There was a time] when I would eat as far out of my comfort zone as a daredevil, just so that I could tell friends I drank live cobra blood. I don't do that anymore," he says. And he wouldn't recommend you try it either.

"I was either going to go to science, engineering, all that, or an art school . . . To me, there seemed to be no difference in the kind of creativity and imagination that goes into either of those areas. I thought, They're equivalent."

—DAVID BYRNE, MUSICIAN

CHAPTER TWO

Where Does Creativity Come From?

n 1930 Albert Einstein wrote that the impulse to wonder about the unknown "is the source of all true art and science." Where does that impulse reside? Scientists haven't figured that out yet. Maybe it's locked in the myriad patterns of synapses—the spaces and connections between brain cells. Maybe it's something external to us—a divine spark or an emergent consciousness. Or maybe it's hiding in our dreams, waiting for us to fall asleep so it can be properly placed in the circular files of the mind. How funny would that be!

Einstein, perhaps the most creative man of the 20th century, was hardly a "normal" person—and the world was better off for it. Then again, what does it mean to be a normal human being? If we can be sufficiently self-aware to cast aside our preconceived notions of the characteristics that define typical people, entire new realms of discovery and creativity may spring forth from new directions. That sure sounds good for us all—and it sure feels good, too.

Children's creativity is incited by their untamed imagination.

$E=MC^2$

StarTalk Live!: Big Brains at BAM [Part 3]

What Is the Neural Basis of Creativity?

Biologically, creativity is essential for human survival. If we run into a life-threatening situation that we've never experienced or heard about before, we need to be able to improvise a solution on the fly. Creativity, in our fight or flight mode, has enabled us to make it this far as a species.

So our brains must have developed some kind of wiring that specifically supports creative activity. How exactly might that work? Let Dr. Heather Berlin, neuroscientist, explain: "What we find is that, whether it's jazz improv or comedy improv, there's a certain neural signature involved when people are improvising. So you can put people in a scanner, even freestyle rappers, and you give them a memorized rap, and then they can freestyle. Or you give a musician a memorized piece or they improv. And when they're improvising . . . a part of the medial prefrontal cortex becomes extra-activated, and that has to do with internally generated ideas. And the dorsal lateral part of the prefrontal cortex becomes deactivated, and that has to do with sort of self-awareness and monitoring your behavior. So you almost go into this free-flowing state. If you become too aware, you mess up, you're not good at improvising. You have to kind of lose yourself, so to speak." ■

The brain turns on self-awareness to generate pure improvisation.

"I wrote a paper on the physiology of laughter in college. It was all wrong, but I wrote the [bleep] out of it."

—EUGENE MIRMAN, COMEDIAN

THINK ON THIS ▶ Does Talent Come Naturally?

True genius unquestionably exists. Some people can just do things the rest of us can't, no matter how hard we try. Many people think, though, that natural talent isn't enough—or, maybe, hardly even matters. Time, practice, and experience, they argue, are the key. "What we associate with Mozart's genius is stuff that he produces 14, 15 years into his life as a composer, which is a fascinating and sobering thought," says author Malcolm Gladwell.

"I think the greatest art allows you to walk up to it and say, 'That means something to me' regardless of what the artist thought or felt."

—DR. NEIL DEGRASSE TYSON, ASTRO-ARTIST-IST

The Science of Creativity With David Byrne

Does Science Inspire Art?

Science is a major human endeavor by which we explore the unknown, and it always has and always will inspire art. The connection goes both ways: How many of today's inventions were first conceived in a science-fiction book, movie, or television show?

Here's a variation on the question: Can we apply purely scientific principles to a "soulless" system and produce art? For example, can we program a computer to compose music? Electronic composer Dr. David Cope thinks so: "The first [computer] program that brought a lot of notoriety was written in about 1980. It's a program called Experiments in Musical Intelligence, and it . . . takes a database of music by typically a classical composer (because they're dead and they can't sue me for imitating their style) . . . and analyzes that music, and fundamentally tries to create a new composition in the style of that music." ∎

Da Vinci's mathematical art

TOUR GUIDE

Can Science and Art Together Achieve Greater Innovations?

"Whenever someone has an understanding of what people really like to do, what they really want to do, they can make good technologies."—Clive Thompson, author of *Smarter Than You Think*

In a college commencement speech, Apple co-founder Steve Jobs credited a college calligraphy class for inspiring his revolutionary work on the first Macintosh computers.

"I still kind of think like an artist," says Biz Stone, co-founder of Twitter. "When I build systems, I think of how it will make people feel, and how they will make others feel."

THINK ON THIS ▶ Is Science Your Muse?

"If I use the word 'nova,' I'll be speaking about a star—unlike the average rapper, who will probably be talking about a car," GZA, co-founder of Wu-Tang Clan, tells us. Of course, both nonscientific and scientific views of the cosmos can inspire artistic expression: "The wonder for the universe happens to a person only when they get out on a clear night . . . and they're starstruck . . . and that's the moment I want to try to communicate," says musician David Crosby.

Is There a Science to Comedy?

This is a question that Neil has asked nearly every comedian who has been on *StarTalk*. While they might not agree on a single formula, each of them takes the craft very seriously and applies a version of the scientific method. Except for Joan Rivers . . . You can read what she says for yourself.

"Comedy is all about math, too. It's all about having the correct amount of words . . . There's the correct amount of words to make a joke perfect. And once it's there, it's done. You're done with that joke; move on to the next one."

LARRY WILMORE

"There is a science to a joke. And one of the things that you'll find . . . [is that] the longer the setup, the harder it is for you to get the payoff. So the shorter the setup, the bigger the payoff. That is, if it's funny."

CHUCK NICE

"Al Jean, who's been running [The Simpsons] for years . . . comedy is like math to him. The script becomes this equation that he's figured out, that pays off in the right places."

HANK AZARIA

"I think that stand-up is very much the scientific method . . . You go onstage; you try something. If it works, you keep it; if it fails, you switch it out."

EUGENE MIRMAN

"For me, as an actor and as a scientist, what I'm aware of is, we're constantly scanning and tracking . . . It's a very complicated process by which I need to make you feel something, I need to make you believe something, and I need every single person to feel that. So, if you're a stand-up, you're working with a room of people. When I work in front of a live audience, I need everyone to feel something. And it's a really complicated interaction."

MAYIM BIALIK

"Anyone who thinks they've gotten it down to ones and zeros has lost what makes comedy great. With that said . . . when you rewrite sketches, just by trial and error you can sort of say, 'Hey, as somebody who's seen 500 sketches, I will just tell you that [works]' . . . There's a little bit of experimentation and finding results and sort of tracking them, but they're not absolute rules."

SETH MEYERS

"Comedy is not controllable, because you can think something is funny and nobody else does . . . But geometry you can control: This to that equals this . . . You can't change it, and I can't change it, and that's it . . . Comedy is not geometry. It is not a science. There's no such thing as the science of comedy. And people that try to teach it, I feel are so cruel."

JOAN RIVERS

"You're going to find structure and science is more in the sitcom realm, because it's setup, delivery, punch, setup, delivery, punch. It's formulaic. In sketch comedy, it's less formulaic; it's more absurdist. You're never really sure of an ending, so you're not so conscious of bringing the scene to a peak, and then . . . an anticlimax, and then finishing it on a climax . . . Sketch comedy is much more ephemeral . . . Of course the purest form is [improv at] Second City. Second City is mercury rolling across the table and splitting up into little balls. Sitcom or film is more of a structured, molecular picture, where you're actually designing and confining things."

DAN AYKROYD

Emoticons are a shortcut for expressing feelings.

OK, So Tell Me: How Did That Make You Feel?

Scientists have divided emotion into seven different categories:

▶ **HAPPINESS** Scientists consider joy the most basic component of happiness; facial expressions of joy can be recognized across every social and cultural group.

▶ **SADNESS** Grief—the mental suffering due to loss or pain—underpins sadness, which can range from disappointment to heartache to despair.

▶ **ANGER** This feeling of dissatisfaction comes usually when some sort of wrongdoing has been perceived.

▶ **SURPRISE** The fundamental component of surprise is the suddenness of the emotion.

▶ **FEAR** The "fight or flight" emotion causes a massive release of adrenaline, instantly raising heart rate, blood pressure, strength, speed, and sensory acuity.

▶ **DISGUST** Eyes crinkle, noses wrinkle, the upper lip pulls up, and the lower lip loosens when we say, "Eww!"

▶ **CONTEMPT** Likely the combination of anger and disgust, contempt is directed toward lower-status entities. ■

"What's interesting when you study the way faces express emotion across cultures, there's extraordinary similarity. An angry person in one culture looks like an angry person in another culture."

—DR. NEIL DEGRASSE TYSON, ASTRO-PISSED-ICIST

THINK ON THIS ▶ **How Far Can a Good Joke Take You?**

Thanks to the speed of radio waves and the vast distances to other stars, anything broadcast today moves outward from Earth at the rate of nearly six trillion miles per year. "If you parked next to Arcturus tonight, which is up in our sky, you would be hearing radio broadcasts or TV from 40 years ago," says Carter Emmart, astronomer and artist. So you better make sure your jokes are still worth listening to a long time from now.

StarTalk Live!: Big Brains at BAM (Part 1)

Funny Ha-Ha or Funny Strange?

Neuroscientist Mayim Bialik may be best known for her role as Amy in the television sitcom *The Big Bang Theory,* known for the quirky humor generated by its even quirkier characters. So what would she say about them?

"All of our characters are, in theory, on the neuropsychiatric spectrum . . . I think what's interesting and kind of sweet—and what I think should not be lost on people—is that we don't pathologize our characters. We don't talk about medicating them or even really changing them . . . This is a group of people who likely were teased, mocked, told that they will never be appreciated or loved . . . who have successful careers, active social lives that involve things like Dungeons & Dragons and video games—but they also have relationships, and that's a fulfilling and satisfying life." ∎

Neil clicks with the characters of The Big Bang Theory.

BACK TO BASICS

What Is Savant Syndrome?

Savant syndrome is a psychological condition in which you may have a mental handicap in one or more significant ways and yet you can perform some cognitive functions at almost superhuman levels. The most common kind of savant you hear about is calendrical: Name any date in the past, and they can tell you what day of the week it was. Mathematical savants can make certain calculations in their head rapidly and flawlessly. Musical savants might be able to play Beethoven sonatas perfectly by ear. Although about half of the time, savant syndrome appears in people who are on the autistic spectrum, scientists still have almost no idea how or why it appears.

THINK ON THIS ▶ What Is Visual Thinking?

Dr. Temple Grandin, a renowned animal scientist and autism activist, has been formally diagnosed with autism spectrum disorder. She explains that her type of photo-realistic thinking is one of the ways that the autistic brain can differ from the typical brain. It allowed her to "get into the head of cattle," noticing how they feared shadows and reflections, which everybody else had missed. "My mind thinks kind of like Google for images," she says.

"We don't see any reason to make that line between kids and adults and play. [Kids] are understanding their world through these adventures that they're having, the little experiments."

—JAMIE HYNEMAN, COHOST OF *MYTHBUSTERS*

CHAPTER THREE

Shall We Play a Game?

Let's pretend. What we do right now won't be for keeps—we'll take a break from the real world, and we won't have to deal with the consequences of our actions. How 'bout it?

I'm sorry. I'm afraid we can't do that. Everything's real these days, even the virtual world; we can't tell the difference between real and imaginary any longer. Technology is confusing the artificial with the natural. Our favorite sports are getting too vicious to play. And even our minds and our senses play tricks with us as we encounter optical illusions, hoaxes, and digital realities that warp our senses and perception of our surroundings.

Well, in that case, let's play in real life. We'll have fun while we figure out how the universe works. We'll use video games to improve our social skills. We'll observe science in action as tilted cars zip by. We'll ride on rising and falling waves of metal. And we'll watch how our entertainment media can make the world a better place. Let's go!

Video games offer endless virtual entertainment.

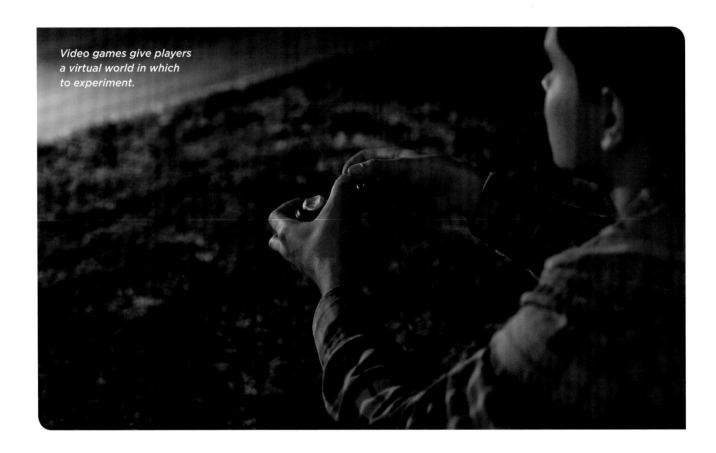

Video games give players a virtual world in which to experiment.

Advancing to the Next Level: The Science of Video Games (Part 1)

Can Video Games Create Violent People?

Tablets and smartphones make gaming mobile.

Since time immemorial, games and sports have been designed to train children for real life. It's probably an extension of the animal kingdom, where tiger cubs and wolf pups wrestle in training for real hunting. Are the games of today really so different from those of yesteryear? "It's interesting that kids, in the absence of video games, used to play Cowboys and Indians, or Cops and Robbers," says Will Wright, designer of *The Sims*.

In our time, parents and policymakers have worried about one bad influence after another: comic books, television shows, rap music, football, and, of course, video games. There is no scientific consensus about whether video games cause their players to act out in real life what they do on the screen. In fact, researchers and social experts are still actively studying the real-life effects of prolonged exposure to both peaceful and violent fictional behaviors experienced through video and computer games. Until then, as with most things, moderation and reasonable limits seem to be the way to go. ∎

What's Real and What's Virtual?

I n the early days of video games, even the simplest simulations were virtual versions of reality that pulled kids in. "I must have been 9 or 10," Elon Musk says of his childhood Commodore VIC-20 home computer. "You construct a little universe . . . You can actually make things happen. You can type these commands, and then something happens on the screen. That's pretty amazing."

One of the first smash arcade video games was *Asteroids* (1979), where the player blasted space rocks and flying saucers to survive. "I spent way too much of my childhood playing that game," remembers astrophysicist Dr. Amy Mainzer. "And so when I became an asteroid scientist, it turns out the game is actually not that bad. If you hit an asteroid that is big in the game, it breaks into a lot of little pieces. And sure enough, that is exactly what happens."

Today, we use remote controlled drones and virtual simulations to train everyone from military personnel to airline pilots to astronauts. "They're still playing these games," says *The Sims* designer Will Wright. "And I know a lot of them are using them for teamwork exercise." ∎

> *"Even in Iraq, after they've gone and done their patrol, they come back to their tent and play* Counter-Strike *on their Xbox."*
>
> —WILL WRIGHT, DESIGNER, *THE SIMS,* ON SOLDIERS PLAYING WAR-BASED VIDEO GAMES

TOUR GUIDE

Did a Video Game Actually Pass the Turing Test?

In 1950, computer scientist Alan Turing suggested a test for artificial intelligence: AI succeeded, or passed the test, when a human couldn't tell if answers to questions were coming from a man or machine. "There was something about 10 years ago called *Starship Titanic* by Douglas Adams," says Jeffrey Ryan, video game expert. "It was designed to have a free-flowing [text] conversation with you . . . In fact, they had Monty Python guys come in to work on it, to make sure the humor [worked]. It passed the Turing test for a little bit."

THINK ON THIS ▶ Can Playing Video Games Increase Your EQ?

"The most educational video game that ever was might have been something like *The Sims*," says video game expert Jeffrey Ryan. "Because think about how often you talk to other people in life and actually have the same sort of interactions." Training you to be socially aware might be upping your "emotional quotient," or EQ.

"We say this at the end of our touring show: that someone once said that the phrase that typifies real discovery is not 'Eureka!' but 'Oh, that's funny.'"

—ADAM SAVAGE, COHOST OF *MYTHBUSTERS*

`MythBusters (Part 1)`

Is Science Just Playing Without the Rules?

Scientists do follow some rules they have created and agreed on—the need to test their hypotheses, for example, with experiments and observations. Overall, though, science is trying to learn the rules of nature—and to have fun doing it. As the hosts of TV's *MythBusters* assert, playing around and trying out new ideas captures the essence of scientific discovery.

"It was somewhere in the second season we realized, wow, actually the structure of the show works best when we are having the most fun," says cohost Adam Savage.

Cohost Jamie Hyneman agrees: "You look at a kid playing and you figure they're just doing it because they're having fun, but they're understanding their world through these little adventures that they're having, these little experiments. It's often very nonlinear, but they're building a foundation of understanding of the world. And there's not really that much difference as far as adults go. A lot of scientists go in this linear direction, and there are times that that's the way to do things and that's very productive, but a lot of the most important discoveries that have been made have been off to the side on some tangent." ∎

Inquisitive kids may have more fun.

BACK TO BASICS

Can You Teach Science Using Rap?

From homage to Sir Mix-A-Lot ("I like Big Bang, and I cannot lie!") to a rap battle between Neil and a flat-Earth believer, rap readily lends itself to science. "It got me where I am now, says GZA, co-founder of Wu-Tang Clan, "because it all started with us studying lessons . . . Some of the lessons related to earth science, like 'What makes rain, hail, snow, earthquakes?' . . . The circumference of the planet, light traveling at 186,000 miles per second—these were [what] we studied coming up, so it kind of gave us an edge on being lyrical, with the wordplay, and flowing, just knowing things, word for word, and started us on our adventure to learn more about the universe."

Rapping isn't just about rhyming words. Building a knowledge base is a necessary first step, explains educator Dr. Christopher Emdin. "Analogy, metaphor, drawing connections, weaving stories . . . The more prolific the MCs, the more complex the lyrics are. The more complex the lyrics are is based on the ability to make connections that the layperson can't see, which is inherently scientific."

Shower songsters exploit the prime acoustics.

Why Do We All Sound Good Singing in the Shower?

"There's no half singing in the shower. You're either an opera diva or a rock star. There's no James Taylor in the shower . . . It's all or nothing in the shower."

—JOSH GROBAN, MUSICIAN

The acoustical properties of a shower stall produce a feedback loop for any singer. It's like having six echoes coming back at you with every note you sing. "It's a pretty epic reverb in the shower," says musician Josh Groban. "That's like a karaoke reverb in there. No one sounds bad in the shower."

There's more to it, though. The sound of the water spray creates a white-noise screen that masks out-of-tune notes and less pleasant frequencies, so only the singer's prettiest primary tones come through. (Listen to a school chorus through the door of the music room for a similar effect.)

Here's another factor to consider—the psychological one. With all the noise in the shower, you can't hear the outside world, and it seems like the outside world can't hear you either. That can remove the singer's inhibitions. Voice teachers will attest that everyone sounds better when singing more confidently, when being self-conscious isn't an issue. So that means you're not the only one who thinks you sound better in the shower. ■

"My whole body below my neck went numb, and I just remember lying there, praying to God that I would be able to get up again and walk."

—CORY BOOKER, U.S. SENATOR

StarTalk Live! at the Apollo (Part 1)

Why Is Football So Dangerous?

I f it weren't for the violence, would American football still be a great game? The skill, strategy, and athleticism of the sport is beautiful, to be sure. But the devastating injuries to all body parts have become a dominant feature of the sport. The invisible wounds of football may be even more frightening; a well-meaning effort to protect the athletes decades ago appears to have led to the medical crisis of chronic traumatic encephalopathy (CTE).

"Football has the greatest concussion rate, and it's because we have the helmets," explains Dr. Ainissa Ramirez, materials scientist and co-author of *Newton's Football*. "The reason we had helmets to begin with is that people used to die from the game. They died because they had skull fractures. In the 1950s [face masks] became standard issue. What that did is change the way we tackle. We used to tackle with our shoulders; then we started tackling with our heads. By putting on the face mask, the helmet became weaponized. So that's what gave rise to concussions." ■

Football helmets have led to more lethal collisions.

BACK TO BASICS

What Can NASCAR Teach Us About Physics?

Every college physics major has been assigned at least one homework problem about auto racetracks. Physics manifests itself in just about every facet of auto racing, from the tilt angle of the track to turn speeds to fuel consumption to burning out the victory doughnuts. "If you are driving at the right speed for that bank, you do not have to turn the steering wheel; the track will turn you," says astro-steering-ist Dr. Neil deGrasse Tyson. "So as far as the car is concerned, it's going in a straight line. They don't ever have to turn the steering wheel to bank those turns . . . So that's a car driving in a straight line with the space-time continuum of the NASCAR track curving its path."

DID YOU KNOW
NASCAR vehicles routinely exceed 200 miles an hour in events at superspeedways like Daytona International Speedway, where the track bank angles range from 18 to 31 degrees.

How Do Roller Coasters Work?

Roller coasters do what their name implies: The wheels roll, and the cars coast—that is, the cars have no independent means of propulsion. All the motion comes from the conversion of the car's gravitational potential energy to kinetic energy and back again, over and over, as the car goes up and down.

The farther up from Earth's surface an object goes, the more gravitational potential energy it has. Once released, the object falls, and its potential energy starts to change into kinetic energy—the

"The highest point of a roller coaster essentially determines the fastest speed you will ever reach on that roller coaster, because it's all about energy."

—DR. NEIL DEGRASSE TYSON

steeper the drop, the faster the conversion goes. Throughout their ride, the cars must overcome the friction of the wheels, which will slow them down.

Finally, if the roller coaster has a vertical loop, the car has to be moving fast enough so that the centrifugal force it feels will pin the car to the track—even when it's upside down. The loops are also not circular—they're stretched vertically to have a steeper drop on the way down but also to make the car's ride smoother as it exits the loop. ∎

A sculpted walkway in Duisburg, Germany, mimics a roller coaster.

Internet trolls hide in anonymity.

The Digital Revolution With Arianna Huffington

What Are Trolls, and Why Do They Exist?

The kind of troll you don't need to fear

Internet trolls use crude insults and foul language to turn online discussions into unpleasant bouts of usually anonymous electronic shouting. In many ways, trolls are like schoolyard and workplace bullies—and their behavior can range from poking fun at people to dangerous threats of violence. Publisher Arianna Huffington explains how to deal with them: "Trolls are incredibly ingenious, some of them. They want to basically have no other life except to circumvent this technology . . . There is something about anonymity that brings the worst out in people . . . Don't feed the trolls. Don't give them attention. Don't reward them. Don't laugh. Because you're giving them what they want." ■

DID YOU KNOW

In a survey of adult Internet users, 28 percent of the respondents admitted to researchers they had engaged in trolling—and most of them were men.

A Conversation With Nichelle Nichols

Can Television Fit Racism?

Can Television Fight Racism?

" I had a man at one of the *Star Trek* conventions in London, where they had the skinheads movement . . . Here was this man, at the front of the line, he couldn't have been more than 18 or 19, but he looked more frightening, with the skin head and the whole thing and the muscles and the tattoos, and he walked over to the table, and my security team tensed . . . and he said, 'I'm not really here as a fan, Miss Nichols. I just wanted you to know that because of you on *Star Trek,* I stopped being what I was on my way to be, and I came here dressed as I had been doing, so that you would know.' This guy is tearing up, and I'm looking up at him tearing, and he said, 'I can never be that again . . . I understand what the world and the future is, and *Star Trek* depicts it, and it's not what I was going through with all my pain and my life. I've done some dastardly things. I can only hope to make up for it.' And I stood, and I leaned across the table . . . and I said, 'Come here, son.' And I put my arms out, and tears came down his eyes, mine, and I held him. And I said, 'Don't look for forgiveness anywhere. God just forgave you. Your choice makes you whole.' And he thanked me, and he walked away, and I turned to my security, and they just stood there like their hands were just limp, and one man said, 'Well, I'll be damned.' And I said, 'No, you'll be blessed. You just got blessed.' "
—Nichelle Nichols, actress who played Lieutenant Uhura on *Star Trek* ■

DID YOU KNOW
Hikaru Sulu was shown as the staff physicist in the pilot episode of *Star Trek* but served as helmsman throughout the rest of the series.

Star Trek's original cast in 1966

"That vision that [Gene Roddenberry, creator of Star Trek] had: starship Enterprise, a metaphor for starship Earth. And the strength of the starship lay in its diversity, coming together and working in concert. Nobody was thinking that."
—GEORGE TAKEI, ACTOR WHO PLAYED HIKARU SULU, HELMSMAN OF THE STARSHIP *ENTERPRISE* ON *STAR TREK*

"It's why we all exist. It's why all living things exist. It is an astonishing fact that on this planet the laws of physics got channeled through this remarkable process, Darwin's evolution by natural selection, to produce objects like us."

—DR. RICHARD DAWKINS, EVOLUTIONARY BIOLOGIST

CHAPTER FOUR

If We Evolved From Monkeys, Why Are Monkeys Still Here?

Few theories in science are as controversial—and as misunderstood—as evolution by natural selection. The process doesn't make us better; it makes us different. And it does so reluctantly, in fits and starts, and agonizingly slowly. It can work really well, and keep a living organism around for a really long time, and then—boom! Its inability to keep that same organism alive is painfully displayed as yet another species bites the dust.

Yes, humans evolved from monkeys. But whether or not you agree, evolutionarily speaking we're not better than monkeys; we're different. There are still monkeys because they evolved to live in trees (where they sure are better off than we would be). We would all do well to remember this fundamental tenet of evolution. It would help us understand who we are, what we are, and where we're headed—whether it's into space or in front of the TV.

Humans and gorillas split from a common ancestor millions of years ago.

DID YOU KNOW
More than 99.9 percent of all species of life that ever existed on Earth have gone extinct. Even so, there are some eight million species currently alive.

StarTalk Live!: Evolution With Richard Dawkins (Part 1)

What Is Darwin's Theory of Natural Selection?

Evolutionary biologist Richard Dawkins uses computers to explain reproduction and evolution: "There is highly accurate, high-fidelity information, really like a computer language, which is copied from generation to generation, and within each generation programs the development of the body in which it sits. Therefore, the fate of the program is bound up in the fate of the body in which it sits."

In every living organism on Earth, just such a computer program runs, coded with the creature's DNA. If the program is successful, the organism can reproduce, and the program survives in the offspring. If the original program isn't perfectly copied, the new organisms are different. If that change helps those new organisms reproduce, then those changed programs survive in the next generation. The process repeats—until, thousands of generations later, the result is the amazing variations of life found on Earth today. ∎

One of Darwin's finches, unique to the Galápagos Islands

BACK TO BASICS

David Attenborough Explains the Mystery of Life

"You can chronicle the history of life in a surprisingly detailed way in quite a short period. You know that life starts in the deep sea, and it leads to different types of invertebrates and shell, and crustaceans and shrimps and so on. Then there are fish with backbones, and fish with backbones emerge onto land and become amphibians with wet skins, and amphibians with wet skins get dry skins and become reptiles. And some of the reptiles turn their scaly skins into feathers and become birds, and the others turn them into hairs and become mammals . . . That's what the history is, and you can put as much or as little detail on that skeleton as you like."—Sir David Attenborough, naturalist

"We've seen it, in a human lifetime: a new species of insect come into being. You make predictions with theories, and here it happens."

—BILL NYE THE EVOLUTION GUY,
ON THE LONDON UNDERGROUND MOSQUITO

Cosmic Queries: Primate Evolution

Are We More Like Bananas or Chimps?

More than half of your DNA is identical to the DNA in a banana. Humans and mushrooms are genetically more alike with one another than either is genetically akin to any green plants. In fact, we share pretty big proportions of genetic material with many different organisms. ■

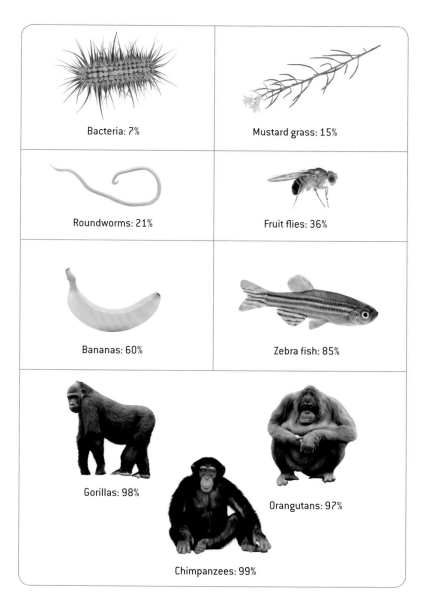

Bacteria: 7%

Mustard grass: 15%

Roundworms: 21%

Fruit flies: 36%

Bananas: 60%

Zebra fish: 85%

Gorillas: 98%

Orangutans: 97%

Chimpanzees: 99%

BIOGRAPHY

👓

Why Was Charlie D. So Awesome?

Born to a wealthy and well-educated English family, Charles Darwin (1809–1882) dutifully followed his parents' wishes to study medicine and religion. Science was his calling, though, and after college, he took the opportunity to sail around the world for nearly five years as ship's naturalist aboard the H.M.S. *Beagle*. His travels, collections, and writing made him a respected naturalist by the time he came home to England. Darwin developed his theory of evolution for 18 years without publishing it, knowing the controversy it would create. Finally a younger colleague, Alfred Russel Wallace, announced he had come up with a similar theory. The two presented their work at the same time, and a year later Darwin published his seminal book, *On the Origin of Species by Means of Natural Selection*.

"Really, he just was jammin', looking at his collections and reaching amazing conclusions, world-changing conclusions. Gotta respect that."

—BILL NYE THE JAMMIN' GUY

Evolution on Earth

Looking at the complexity of life on Earth today, it's tempting to believe that something or someone had to plan it all out. But there was no need; just put together enough DNA, environmental conditions, and time, and a set of environmental stressors—and it all happens naturally.

|||||||
Eyes

◀ The evolutionary path from clusters of photosensitive cells to organs that produce detailed images has happened independently in the animal kingdom dozens of times. Octopus eyes, for example, don't have the "blind spot" human eyes have, because their optic nerve fibers are located behind the retina.

|||||||
Echolocation

◀ Dolphins are swimming mammals, and bats are flying ones—yet each developed the ability to hunt prey by emitting high-pitched sounds and listening to their echoes. Research suggests that they each evolved that ability independently but based on the same genetic mutations.

|||||||
Wolf to Pomeranian

◀ Thousands of generations of evolution and breeding have transformed wolves from a frightening and fierce predator into the full spectrum of domesticated dogs—including cute and cuddly little toy varieties.

Stingers

▲ Female insects often deposit their eggs using a penetrating appendage in their abdomens. Worker bees, which are all female, have a similar organ—but it deposits venom as a weapon in defense of its hive's egg layer, the queen.

Giraffes

◀ Unlike apatosaurs or barosaurs, which evolved more and longer vertebrae, giraffes have the same number of neck bones as humans. Variations in those neck bones led to both short-necked and long-necked giraffes over millions of years.

Primates

◀ The first protoprimates appeared on Earth just as the dinosaurs went extinct. About 15 million years ago, the great apes began their evolutionary fragmentation, splitting into the four types that survive today: orangutans, gorillas, chimps, and us.

Homo sapiens versus Homo neanderthalis

▲ For years, we thought Neanderthals were our ancient ancestors (most of us have some Neanderthal DNA)—until scientific testing showed they most likely represent a different branch of our hominid family.

FUTURES IMAGINED

Zombies! Superheroes! Warp drive! Aliens! And, maybe most fantastical of all, time travel! As Albert Einstein wrote: "Imagination embraces the entire world, stimulating progress, giving birth to evolution. It is, strictly speaking, a real factor in scientific research." We can't always create what we imagine. But we also can't intentionally create what we don't imagine first. Science fiction looks at the best and the worst of humanity—the endless possibilities of Earth and space—and that mind's eye will forever push the boundaries of "what is" toward "what could be." So let's go to the limit—and then zip on by!

"It's their biological imperative to spread the virus. Through the eating, they're not ingesting nutrition, but it is an act that is familiar to their DNA. They already know how to eat, and that's the best way to spread the virus. They are a walking plague. They are literally a virus."

—MAX BROOKS, AUTHOR OF *WORLD WAR Z*

CHAPTER ONE

When Are the Zombies Coming?

Mindless. Unstoppable. Terrifying! Zombies are all the rage, taking over not only in horror films (*28 Days Later*) and on TV (*The Walking Dead*) but also sci-fi conventions (*Night of the Living Trekkies*), math class (*Zombies and Calculus*), and Victorian literature (*Pride and Prejudice and Zombies*).

Modern zombies are fictional, but the zombie phenomenon is really an allegory about plagues, death, and the end of civilized society. And the microscopic pathogens that can cause such disasters are all too real. As technology advances into medicine, it seems all too likely that we could sow the seeds of our own destruction, either biologically with experiments on viruses and germs, or mechanically with artificial nano-invaders.

Don't despair. Through scientific research and medicine, we are starting to peer into the fiction and extract the reality. And with that knowledge will come power—the ability to eradicate disease, and to harness viruses to do much more good than harm.

Zombies have been imagined many ways but are nearly always murderous and bloodthirsty.

Zombie Apocalypse (Part 2)

Could Zombies Actually Exist?

Humanity's view of zombies has changed over the years. In fantastical antiquity, as depicted in swords-and-sorcery games like Dungeons & Dragons, a zombie was a magical "undead" creature, similar to a vampire or lich. About a century ago, popular accounts of zombies in Haiti described them as reanimated human corpses controlled by evil voodoo necromancers—or, alternatively, as "zombified" living people under the influence of psychoactive drugs. Science-fiction zombies entered the mainstream with Hollywood B movies like *Plan 9 From Outer Space* (1959, considered by some to be the worst film ever made) and *Night of the Living Dead* (1968).

Today's fictional zombies are biological, created by an infectious virus, and are even deadlier than those of decades ago. They're not only hard to kill, but they have an insatiable appetite for human flesh, and their bite would infect you with their zombieness—ensuring that you'll wind up just like them upon your demise. From video games like *Resident Evil* to novels like *World War Z*, each zombie depiction is more vicious and bloodthirsty than the last. We know that some dreaded diseases, like rabies, can be passed along through saliva, but it takes weeks for symptoms to develop, not seconds. So while some kind of zombie germ may be conceivable, it's a stretch. ∎

The rise of movies like this inspired zombie fever.

"When something bites you, you don't turn into that thing . . . If that were remotely possible, Evander Holyfield would have turned into Mike Tyson years ago."

—DR. NEIL DEGRASSE TYSON, ASTRO-NEVER-HEARD-OF-WEREWOLVES-IST

THINK ON THIS ▶ What Do Zombie Fantasies Say About Society?

"I think the reason the zombie craze is so crazy right now is because we're living in such anxiety-ridden times . . . It's the one apocalyptic scenario in which we can feel empowered. You cannot hit a credit default swap in the head . . . If you keep a cool head and, as the British say, keep calm and carry on, you'll be all right."
—Max Brooks, author of *World War Z*

DID YOU KNOW

In *World War Z,* author Max Brooks introduced a concept called the "resource-to-kill ratio," which is "literally how much resources you have to use to kill one zombie, because it becomes a war of economics."

Cosmic Queries: Viruses, Outbreaks, and Pandemics

Is There Really a Zombie Fungus?

It's true. There's a zombie fungus on the loose! Sort of. "I don't know that we've actually seen a fungus that turned people into zombies, but we certainly see fungi that execute all kinds of clever activities to force the behavior of whatever they infect to facilitate spread of their spores," says science journalist Laurie Garrett. "You might argue that's what athlete's foot in a gym is."

There are indeed parasitic fungi out there: Alfred Russel Wallace, the famous British naturalist who pioneered the theory of evolution by natural selection with Charles Darwin, discovered *Ophiocordyceps unilateralis,* a parasitic fungus that infects tropical tree ants. The infected ant convulses, falls to the jungle floor, and climbs up back toward the treetops. On its way back up, it bites down hard on a leaf, and its mandibles lock in place. Over several days' time, the ant dies. The fungus sprouts through the dead ant's head, and new spores are released to seek their next victims. ∎

BACK TO BASICS

How to Cure Zombies With Salt

Author Mark Kurlansky talked about the treatment of zombies in Haiti: "I have spent a lot of time working in Haiti, so I already knew that salt was used to cure zombies . . . because salt takes away evil . . . If somebody has been zombified, you can bring them back to normal with salt . . . I have to say: I haven't done it. But there is this association with salt preventing evil and curing evil, because it stops rotting."

The Cordyceps *fungus sprouts from a murdered ant.*

"You've heard the phrase 'cat lady'—somebody who owns hundreds of cats and behaves in a very eccentric way? Maybe a lot of those people are infected with this parasite."

—MARC ABRAHAMS, FOUNDER OF THE IG NOBEL PRIZES, ON THE PARASITE *TOXOPLASMA GONDII*

Zombie Apocalypse (Part 1)

How Would a Zombie Virus Spread?

Zombies are particularly wrathful in large numbers.

A virus is merely a bundle of genetic material with an imperative to make copies of itself. Epidemiologists look to both biological disease vectors (like air, water, or blood) and human behavior to make models of how diseases spread.

Max Brooks, author of *World War Z*, says he based his zombie virus on AIDS: "I wanted to make it very hard to get, just like AIDS was very hard to get. And therefore, from a storytelling point of view, the mistakes were made by us. Because the truth is, let's face it, if in 1980 Reagan had gone on TV and said, 'My fellow Americans, there's a disease that's real hard to get, but if you get it, it's going to be really bad. Here's 10 things you can do to avoid it'—boom!—AIDS would have been a paragraph in a medical journal . . . We could have made AIDS extinct with a pamphlet; that's how we could have stopped it."

> "What I love is that you're starting to get genuine thinkers; you're starting to get genuine academics and smart people who are really looking at a zombie plague from an academic point of view."
> —MAX BROOKS, AUTHOR OF *WORLD WAR Z*

"If only that were true," argues epidemiologist Dr. Ian Lipkin. "I don't think a pamphlet would have changed the course." ∎

DID YOU KNOW
In his short story "The Giving Plague," astrophysicist Dr. David Brin describes a virus that compels people to donate blood—it's the only way the virus can spread from one host to another.

LAUGH OUT LOUD ▶ With the U.S. Centers for Disease Control

"Get a Kit—Make a Plan—Be Prepared" reads the poster, with a zombie staring menacingly outward. In 2011, Dr. Ali Khan at the Centers for Disease Control led the distribution of tongue-in-cheek online antizombie materials, including the graphic novel *Preparedness 101: Zombie Pandemic*, to engage teenagers and children with the topic of emergency planning, without getting too serious about disaster and disease. It spurred the largest amount of Internet traffic the CDC has ever had.

PREPAREDNESS 101:
Zombie Pandemic

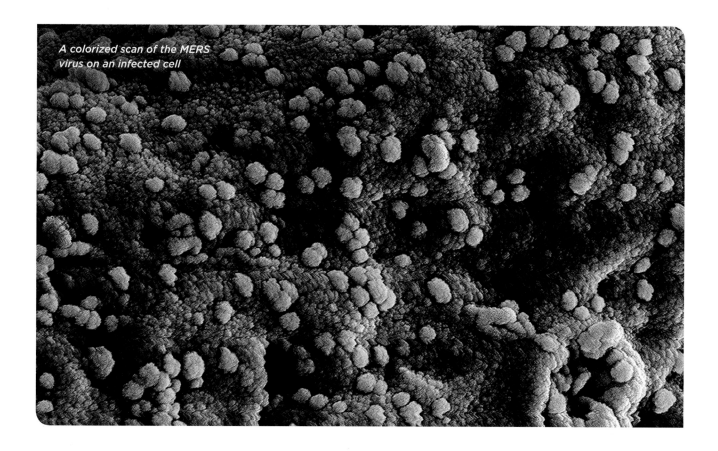

A colorized scan of the MERS virus on an infected cell

`Zombie Apocalypse [Part 1]`

How Do Viruses Really Work?

Viruses that appear spherical are actually icosahedrons.

Though epidemiologist Dr. Ian Lipkin says "a very famous virologist once referred to a virus as a piece of bad news wrapped up in a protein coat," it's unlikely viruses have any conception at all of good or evil. In fact, not all viruses are bad. But they do all work the same: A virus will inject itself into a cell and then hijack its machinery, forcing the cell to make the genetic material and proteins needed to replicate the virus. In other words, a virus can turn a cell into its slave—or zombie!

If the cell's internal immune response isn't strong enough to resist the virus, the cell will die once the virus is done with it. From there, the viral copies will disperse to find the next cells to enslave. And so the virus continues to live, and spread, one cell at a time. ∎

"It's evil beef jerky."
—COMEDIAN EUGENE MIRMAN ON VIRUSES

Zombie Viruses or Real Viruse
What's the Bigger Threat?

In fiction, zombie pandemics are almost always caused by poor behavior
planning on the part of healthy humans. So how does a zombie-virus att
stack up to the thousands—maybe millions—of kinds of real viruses on Ea

|||||||

▼ INCUBATION

Pathogens incubate, or reproduce, for varying
periods of time without the host's showing
symptoms. The longer the incubation period
lasts, the more people can be infected before an
epidemic is noticed. The zombie virus usually
incubates quite quickly.

|||||||

▲ CONTAGION

Viruses like Ebola can travel several feet via
droplets in the air—when, for example, an
infected patient coughs up blood. The zombie
virus can be transferred only by direct contact
and the exchange of bodily fluids.

|||||||

◄ TRANSMISSION

Viruses like measles or influenza can
travel through the air for long distances
and linger in the air for long periods of
time. As long as a zombie doesn't touch
you, you're fine

||||||||

◀ VECTORS

Viruses like dengue fever and Zika are transmitted by mosquitoes—which can travel a long way and carry the virus with them. Zombie viruses can usually only be passed along through humans.

||||||||

▶ MORTALITY

If everyone infected by a virus dies from it, an epidemic could be self-limiting, because there'd be no more carriers left. The zombie virus lives on, though, even after its host dies, so it won't self-limit.

||||||||

▲ FATALITIES

In approximately one year, a MERS epidemic killed about 600 people; SARS, 800 people; Ebola, 11,300 people; the 1918 influenza, about 50 million people. The death toll from all zombie viruses so far: zero.

AND THE WINNER IS . . .

The Top Three Viruses

"If you ask me what bothers me most in terms of the state of the world, it really is HIV," says Dr. Ian Lipkin, epidemiologist. "Number two would be influenza. And number three would be the one I don't know about, because we're seeing new things all the time."

HIV, the virus that causes AIDS, can be transmitted only through direct contact with bodily fluids. Yet because of human behavior, it has reduced life expectancy in some African nations by more than a decade, and it continues to spread rampantly worldwide through unprotected sexual activity and the sharing of infected needles. As for influenza, it mutates so quickly that it continues to kill hundreds of thousands of people each year. ■

Zombie Apocalypse [Part 2]

How Did SARS Spread Around the World?

"Fear does kill in an epidemic. People behave really stupidly and put themselves at great risk," says science journalist Laurie Garrett. "[During] the SARS epidemic, I was in Hong Kong, and there were two major hospitals that the bulk of all of the patients went to . . . It started in China and was covered up. It started in November 2002, [and] we didn't know about it until . . . it hit Hong Kong. And it hit Hong Kong because one individual was infected, was terrified, knew what was going down, because he was a doctor, staggered across the border, went to a hotel called the Metropole in downtown Hong Kong, stayed on the ninth floor, and everybody else on the ninth floor that pressed the 9 button on the elevator got his disease. They were travelers. They went to their respective airport destinations and took the virus— to Vietnam, to Toronto . . ." ∎

A factory worker in Beijing dons a mask to ward off SARS in 2003.

BACK TO BASICS

Can DNA Jump Between Species?

A research project by plant geneticists recently showed that the genome of the common sweet potato contains DNA from a soil bacterium that causes abnormal growths at the root crowns of many trees and shrubs. This isn't the kind of DNA transfer from typical hybridization, but rather much more like naturally occurring genetic modification—GMOs without human intervention.

How might the bacterial DNA have entered into the sweet potato genome? Possibly a virus attacked a sweet potato cell long ago, injecting all kinds of foreign DNA—but the cell survived, thanks to its immune system, and the DNA was incorporated into the cell.

DID YOU KNOW

Modern gene therapy, being developed by doctors to fight cancer and other serious diseases, involves the genetic modification of human cells by introducing outside DNA, sometimes from viruses, and also using viruses to deliver the genetic material.

Combating Disease With Jimmy Carter

Didn't We Already Wipe Out Polio?

DID YOU KNOW
If the global program of polio vaccination and eradication stopped today, the annual number of polio cases worldwide could skyrocket to 200,000 in a single decade. The program costs more than one billion dollars a year to operate.

Polio was one the most feared diseases of the 20th century. This highly contagious viral disease struck without warning, rich and poor alike, and it paralyzed, crippled, and killed hundreds of thousands of people each year. Then, Drs. Jonas Salk and Albert Sabin developed polio vaccines; within a generation, the number of cases in the United States dropped to almost zero.

"The biggest lesson from tuberculosis, HIV, go down the list: You don't want to be part of a disenfranchised group or a group that the larger society looks down upon. Because if you are that individual, society will not be there for you."
—LAURIE GARRETT, SCIENCE JOURNALIST

Today, thanks to an ongoing eradication program, the number of reported cases worldwide dropped from nearly 400,000 in 1988 to barely 100 in 2015. We're not done yet, though. Invertebrate biologist Dr. Mark Siddall explains why: "Right now there's fewer than 500 new cases of polio, but they're in Waziristan, they're in Syria, they're in southern Somalia, and they're in northern Nigeria. These are places of conflict . . . What goes on in a war-torn area is an inability to provide services, and an inability to track cases and find out where they are. Both of those, at the front end and the back end: You lose the connection to health care, and it's devastating." ■

Protruding proteins of the polio virus seek out a host.

"By understanding the science of disease . . . we've been able to preserve the lives of millions of people around the world, raising their quality of life and making them more productive, so that people everywhere enjoy longer, healthier lives. It's wonderful."
—BILL NYE THE PUBLIC HEALTH GUY

"Bending steel with his bare hands—I'm good with that. Flying in blue panty hose—I'm good with that. But taking energy from the Sun? No, no, not in a million years."

—DR. NEIL DEGRASSE TYSON, ASTRO-SUPERHERO-IST

CHAPTER TWO

Could Superman Survive a Black Hole?

What could be more fun than being able to climb up walls, vibrate through walls, or vaporize walls with a glance? Creatures with supernatural powers have appeared throughout history—but costumed superheroes have been part of pop culture for less than a century.

Their debut coincided with our first forays into modern science and technology—the expanding universe, quantum mechanics, transoceanic flights, and more. Superman, unsurprisingly, was an alien; Batman, a science-based detective; and Wonder Woman, an Amazonian who flew an invisible plane. As our knowledge progressed, so did our heroes—like the Fantastic Four, created by cosmic rays; the Hulk, victim of gamma radiation; Firestorm, the nuclear man; and cosmic superheroes Nova and Quasar.

The imaginative pseudoscience that comes from comic books inspires us to ask questions and seek answers while having fun doing it. And of course we wonder: Could we be superheroes too?

Humans can't travel through
a black hole, but could a superhero?

"As he was trying to run at the speed of light, he was going slower . . . It was a beautiful illustration of Einstein's principles."

—DR. JAMES KAKALIOS, AUTHOR OF *THE PHYSICS OF SUPERHEROES*

Hulk may outsize Bruce Banner, but he'd weigh the same.

Cosmic Queries: Superheroes

Would Superman or Mr. Fantastic Survive Spaghettification?

Comic books play fast and loose with the laws of physics, but we don't. "If you can actually travel faster than light, you can just climb out of a black hole; nothing will stop you," says Neil. "However, the journey down to the singularity would, as sure as night follows day, spaghettify him . . . In principle, anybody who is stretchable [like Mr. Fantastic] might be immune to this."

▶ HOW CAN THE HULK GROW AND SHRINK?

"He can't just get bigger, unless he has the same mass," explains Neil. "And if he does, he's less dense in the state of Hulk than he is as Bruce Banner."

"So he'd be very kind of marshmallowy?" asks Chuck Nice.

Sure, says Neil. "Or he'd be like a beach ball."

▶ CAN MAGNETO CONTROL EARTH'S CORE?

"Yes, but just because something's made of metal doesn't mean Magneto can control it, because not all metal is magnetic," Neil clarifies. "Magneto could totally tear a new one in a star, because he can interact with the magnetic fields that control where those gases appear and what they do."

▶ WHAT KEEPS THE FLASH FROM BURNING UP?

The Flash gets his superspeed thanks to a fictional "speed force," which is fundamental to the universe, like gravity. An energy aura permeates and surrounds him as he runs—so he's protected from friction, which would otherwise set him on fire, and he doesn't get squashed if he runs into something at superspeed. ■

Cosmic Queries: Superheroes

Can We Increase Human Attributes, Like Captain America?

Captain America is human and superhuman at the same time. How does he do it? Could we do it, too? "We're all human at the end of the day," admits astro-muscle-ist Dr. Neil deGrasse Tyson. "Muscle size correlates with muscle strength. So you can have a Captain America who, if he had a good body, would turn heads in a fitness center, but the strength of those muscles is not such that he would have the strength exhibited by any genetic manipulation at all—and still have it be biological matter."

> *"Anything that any biological creature does that is special could, in theory, be incorporated into a human being."*
> —DR. LEE SILVER, MOLECULAR BIOLOGIST

There may be one caveat to Neil's explanation, though. If the Super-Soldier Serum changed the way Captain America's muscles are actually put together— that is, he's human, but slightly evolved beyond typical humans—then there could be more tensile strength per muscle fiber in his body, leading to greater strength even with the same size. And remember, he's superstrong for a man, but he's not Hulk-strong or anything. ∎

Patriotic super-soldier Captain America attained peak human performance.

BACK TO BASICS

What Would NOT Happen If a Radioactive Spider Bit You?

The "spider powers" that Peter Parker received from the radioactive spider bite in the original comic books did not include, interestingly, his web. He actually invented both his web fluid and web shooters while he was in high school—either of which would have totally been a winning science-fair project. Although Spider-Man probably wields them better than anyone else, actually anyone with enough practice could use them.

THINK ON THIS ▶ Would We Get Powers If We Used Our Whole Brain?

"The fact is, the idea that we use 10 percent of our brain was never true. It is a misquote from what actually was said by [a] neuroscientist a hundred years ago, who said, 'The brain is so complex we only know what 10 percent of it is used for.' So all this stuff with Professor X [telepathy] . . . and Lucy [telekinesis], this is a fiction." —Dr. Neil deGrasse Tyson, astro-debunk-icist

DID YOU KNOW
In a 2014 survey of Australian children, their five favorite superheroes were Batman, Spider-Man, Superman, Iron Man, and Wonder Woman.

The Physics of Superheroes, the Sequel

Which Superpowers Will Technology Make Possible?

Technology already exists now that can do things superheroes do. Jet-powered wingpacks allow people to fly like an airplane. Backscatter x-ray imagers and active millimeter-wave scanners provide penetrating vision like Superman's. Maybe the most exciting superpower-like advances are in the areas of applied quantum mechanics: Quantum entanglement may someday allow teleportation; quantum computing could produce artificial superintelligence. Theoretical physicist Dr. Michio Kaku thinks that's the case as well: "If you could control the laws of the quantum, then you could in fact have . . . most of the superpowers of science fiction."

The biggest drawback for a lot of this technology is its portability. Can you carry that backscatter x-ray imager on your head as you fly through the air, for example? So these technologies will need to be miniaturized. ∎

NEIL TWEETS

Which Superhero Would Neil Like to Be?

"I like Batman, I can be Batman. And who doesn't like the gadgets? And who doesn't like the car? He's got the best car of any of them…You gotta like the car. He's got cool things that the car can do. So the car is an extension of his utility belt in terms of its coolness factor. So for me, I'd have to be Batman."
—Dr. Neil deGrasse Tyson, astro-bat-icist

"I would have loved to have done Dr. Manhattan in Watchmen. However, I just worked with Billy [Crudup], who played Dr. Manhattan, and he was magnificent."
—LAURENCE FISHBURNE, ACTOR, ON WHICH SUPERHERO HE'D LIKE TO PLAY

Cyclops from X-Men (2000) emits an optic blast through his visor.

The Physics of Superheroes

Could the Invisible Woman Really Disappear?

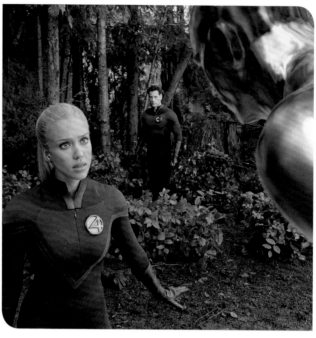

Invisible Woman in Fantastic Four: Rise of the Silver Surfer *(2007)*

In principle, making something invisible is easy: Just bend light from behind the object around it, so that whatever is behind it looks the same. We already know how that can be done in nature: A large concentration of mass—a black hole or a cluster of galaxies, for example, or even the sun in a weaker way—will act as a gravitational lens and bend light accordingly. Out in the universe, though, the lensing effect creates distortion in the shape and brightness of the objects behind it—a dead give-away for an unseen superhero.

A more practical device has now been developed that might work better: a continuously multidirectional 3-D cloaking device. It can work only on small items now—a hand or a face, but not an entire person. Maybe someday, though, portable full-fledged invisibility systems will make the Invisible Woman's power seem like no big deal. (Her force fields, though, would still be quite formidable.) ∎

> "[As a kid] I wanted to be Mighty Mouse. Because I wanted to save women when mean people were trying to harm them. And I wanted to sing opera while I was doing it."
>
> —DR. NEIL DEGRASSE TYSON, ASTRO-RODENT-ICIST

> "We analyzed [Wonder Woman's bracelets] from a materials science point of view . . . What are these bracelets made out of that can deflect bullets? . . . Cold rolled steel would probably be strong enough . . . Of course, her wrists don't snap, so she's excessively strong."
>
> —DR. JAMES KAKALIOS, PHYSICIST AND AUTHOR OF *THE PHYSICS OF SUPERHEROES*

THINK ON THIS ▶ How Does Athletic Wear Impact Superhero Movie Costumes?

"I always look to what sports figures do, and specifically what they do for the Olympics. That's the time when a lot of innovative technical fabrics are introduced for athletes . . . That's how it trickles down then to film. And, for instance, the costume designers for Spider-Man said, 'You know what? That looked really great, speed skaters, so let's appropriate that for the costume.'" —James Aguiar, fashion designer

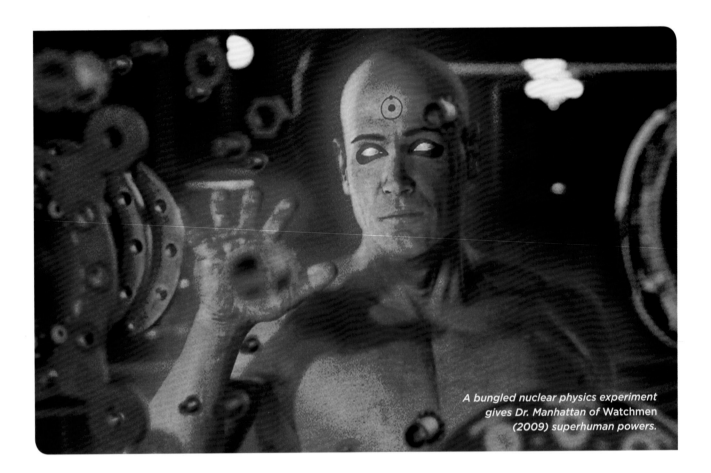

A bungled nuclear physics experiment gives Dr. Manhattan of Watchmen *(2009) superhuman powers.*

Do Superheroes Teach Us Science?

"Mighty Mouse had a cape. Superman had a cape. So to me, it was clear: It was the cape that makes you fly. It was clearly the case . . . This was when I was in third grade or something."

—DR. NEIL DEGRASSE TYSON, ASTRO-CAPE-ICIST

Spider-Man's alter ego, Peter Parker (who shares a name, by the way, with a retired nuclear astrophysics professor at Yale), was a graduate teaching assistant for a semester or so. Seriously, though: In the same way that *Star Trek* communicators and tricorders have inspired mobile phones and medical imagers, superheroes make us think about what we haven't discovered yet.

Take, for example, Neil's desire for powers like that of the blue-skinned Dr. Manhattan: "In *Watchmen,* he has become a macroscopic quantum object, so where he can say, 'I can become this particle-wave duality myself. And I can, at will, become the wave and show up where the wave traveled in another spot and reassemble myself, and there I am.' Why can't we do that?"

Physicist Dr. James Kakalios has a simple explanation: "Because we don't have independent control over our quantum mechanical waves." ∎

Could You Play Quidditch in Space?

Lots of magic users are superheroes—the Scarlet Witch of the Avengers and Zatanna of the Justice League come to mind—but they rarely are much fun. An airborne arena teeming with witches and wizards on broomsticks, though? Now that's a sport. Quidditch may be the greatest game ever invented in fiction and translated into reality—except that the version played in college club leagues today is strictly two-dimensional.

With only minor modifications, though, Chasers, Beaters, Keepers, and Seekers could ply their trade in space—with rocket packs instead of magical brooms. The scoring rings would have to be held in place somehow, presumably affixed to the edges of an orbiting stadium. The players' space suits had better be durable, though—it's all fun and games until somebody loses their airtight seal because a Bludger strike cracks a helmet or visor. ■

"The [Golden] Snitch, of course we presume, doesn't have broom powers but is actually aerodynamically supporting itself with flapping wings, like a hummingbird. Wings are useless in zero g . . . A bird on an airless planet is a brick. So they'd have to redesign the Snitch for that one."

—DR. NEIL DEGRASSE TYSON, ASTRO-QUIDDITCH-IST

BACK TO BASICS

Could We Replace a Skeleton With Metal?

From Wolverine of the X-Men, to Cyborg of the Teen Titans, to the Six Million Dollar Man and the Bionic Woman, exotic internal prosthetics have been the pseudotechnological source of many a superhero's powers. Neil points out what he sees is a flaw with this strategy: "Keep in mind that for the human body to work, you'd have to graft the tissue onto the metal. Our muscles connect to tendons that connect to ligaments that connect to your bones. It works biologically. In order to get foreign material in there, you're gonna have to attach it all some other way."

THINK ON THIS ▶ What If You Had Atomic Powers?

Dr. Solar, Man of the Atom, has been around in various incarnations since 1962. Among other things, he can transmute elements at will. So what could you do with power over the periodic table? Physicist Dr. Michio Kaku explains: "You get gold from nothing." And comedian Chuck Nice is all in: "OK. There you have it. Thank you very much, sir . . . I want that power."

Science Versus Superman

Faster than a speeding bullet! More powerful than a locomotive!
Able to leap tall buildings in a single bound! Just how super is Superman,
subjected to the scrutiny of science? Here are Neil's answers
to the essential questions about Superman.

 ## ▲ DOES HE KNOW ASTRONOMY?

"Superman wanted to find his home planet, Krypton, because the light signal of Krypton, [once it was] destroyed, would be coming to us about now. And he came to the planetarium. So I'm director of the planetarium . . . So I'm there with Superman."

‖‖‖ ◄ SHOULDN'T HE BE RADIOACTIVE?

"You can't store [solar] energy in an unlimited way without getting hot—as in radioactive. It's just how nature manifests itself. He'd be very hot, and you'd know he was coming from a long way."

‖‖‖ ◄ HOW DOES HE FLY?

"What you have to rely on is his muscular strength from a planet that may have a very high surface gravity . . . If you're that strong, it looks like you're flying when you're just leaping."

|||||||
▲ WHO WOULD WIN: SUPERMAN OR THE *ENTERPRISE*?

"I have no doubt that Superman can take the starship *Enterprise* and the entire crew . . . If Superman goes to the tail of the *Enterprise* and punches it or swings it around lasso-style, that's the end."

|||||||
▲ WHAT'S WITH THE YELLOW SUN THING?

"We know the difference between a yellow star and a red star . . . It's just light. So if it's light that gave Superman his powers and if it's red light that took them away, then all you'd need to do is shine red light on Superman and he'd be a crying mess."

|||||||
◀ WHAT'S DEADLIER: HIS GAS OR HIS WIND?

NEIL: There's physics in everything. That's all I'm saying.
CHUCK NICE: I can't tell you how sorry I am that I asked that question . . . I will never get that image out of my head.

"So what's science fiction? Science fiction serves a good purpose. Because it sets those goals, those benchmarks out in nowhere. And we work toward that. And then—now—we surpass that."
—GEORGE TAKEI, ACTOR WHO PLAYED SULU ON *STAR TREK*

(CHAPTER THREE)

Why Don't We Have Flying Cars Yet?

By today, said the science-fiction writers of the 20th century, we all would be zooming around above our cities. Robots would be catering to our every need. And we would be living on other planets and beyond.

We should thank our lucky stars they were wrong. Otherwise, by now we'd be driving desperately around a destroyed society or enslaved by mechanical masters or stranded on distant outposts, yearning for the green shores of our home world. At least we have smartphones, solar panels, search engines, and space stations. It could be a lot worse.

Science fiction points out possibilities for us to ponder. It affects how we think, where we live, when we laugh, and even what we wear. It may try to be realistic, or not. It just has to be believable enough for us to see beyond the fantasy and look to the core of who and what we are. Science fiction allows us to examine ourselves from the outside. Let's peek now at what's inside!

We haven't reached an age of flying cars—but are we close?

Science fiction can be about the future, the past, or both.

What Is Science Fiction?

According to the Gunn Center for the Study of Science Fiction at the University of Kansas, sci-fi is fundamentally "the literature of the human species encountering change." It can inspire, entertain, and warn us about what was, is, and may be.

Science fiction is usually about the future, but it can be about the past—especially in time-travel or alternate-reality stories. And in some cases—like H. G. Wells's novel *The Time Machine* or the 2006 movie *The Fountain*—it can be about both.

▸ WHERE ARE THE FLYING CARS?

"Are you sure you want a flying car?" asks Elon Musk, founder of Tesla Motors and SpaceX. "If there are flying cars, then, well, obviously you've added this additional dimension where now a car could potentially fall on your head."

▸ HOW REAL IS THE SCIENCE IN SCI-FI?

Sometimes, it's right on. Other times, not so much—like Han Solo making the Kessel Run, says Neil. "[A parsec] is a unit of distance, and there he is boasting about the speed of the Millennium Falcon in 12 parsecs. So this is a completely scientifically illiterate statement. Later on, there'd be this revisionist discussion . . . 'Oh, no, what he meant was the Millennium Falcon went past a warp in space-time, making the distance shorter.' " ■

"We had this amazing device that was attached to our hip. And we would walk around with it all the time. And whenever we wanted to talk to someone, we'd rip it off, flip it open, and start talking. At that time, it was an astounding piece of technology. Today we've gone way past that."

—GEORGE TAKEI, ACTOR WHO PLAYED SULU, DESCRIBING *STAR TREK*'S COMMUNICATORS

In the premier episode of Star Trek *(1966) the* Enterprise *crew leave the ship via transporter.*

What Would Actually Happen in a Transporter?

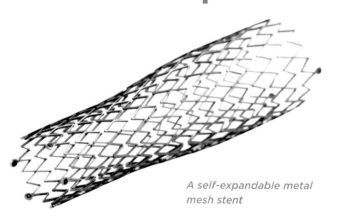

A self-expandable metal mesh stent

In the *Star Trek* transporters, your atoms and their information were recorded, disassembled, sent in an energy beam, and then reassembled at a distant location. "The problem with that is that [if] you convert your mass into energy, that would be an explosion larger than every nuclear bomb on the planet. That would be bad," explains Dr. Phil Plait, astrophysicist and author of *Bad Astronomy: Misconceptions and Misuses Revealed.*

The complexity of transporting goes to the quantum level, too. We all have at least a thousand trillion trillion atoms in our bodies, so scanning and recording even one person's most basic atomic information would far exceed all the current computer storage capacity on Earth.

"How about transporting a stent into your artery so you don't have to do any surgery?" asks Dr. Charles Liu, astrophysicist.

Maybe it's best to start simple, think small, and learn to transport useful but inanimate objects for now. ■

StarTalk and Baba Booey Rock Comic-Con (Part 2)

Could the Death Star Really Blow Up a Planet?

Zapping a planet-size object *Star Wars*–style with a single powerful beam of energy looks great, but it doesn't really work. "It turns out . . . it's almost impossible," admits astrophysicist Dr. Phil Plait. "You could take something the size of Mars and hit the Earth with it, and not completely destroy it. So to completely destroy a planet . . . it takes a huge amount of energy . . . When you calculate it, it's like more energy than the Sun puts out."

The more recent *Star Trek* version of planetary destruction—collapsing the planet with its own gravity into a singularity—makes more sense energy-wise and mass-wise—but it's got reality-check problems of its own, like the utter impossibility of so-called "red matter."

Astro-kablooey-ist Dr. Neil deGrasse Tyson explains: "So you calculate the binding energy of the planet. And if you pump more energy than the binding energy into the planet, it'll explode in the way the Death Star destroys a planet . . . You can destabilize a planet if you make Swiss cheese out of its innards—that's clear. But I like the *Star Wars* style of destruction. Just a good old-fashioned planetary explosion." ■

NEIL TWEETS

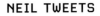

Neil and Brian Cox's Lightsaber Twitter War

@NEILTYSON

> If LightSabers are made of light, they would just pass through one another.

> Not if the photons are sufficiently high energy.

@PROFBRIANCOX

@NEILTYSON

> We could trap the escaping particles within one of the swords.

> The charged particles produced could be magnetically contained.

@PROFBRIANCOX

"Maybe the name is just wrong. Maybe they just call it a lightsaber. That doesn't mean it's made of light."

—DR. PHIL PLAIT, ASTROPHYSICIST AND AUTHOR OF *BAD ASTRONOMY: MISCONCEPTIONS AND MISUSES REVEALED*

THINK ON THIS ▶ How Would a Lightsaber Actually Work?

DR. BRIAN COX: At very high energies—very high-energy collisions—there is a probability that photons will kick off each other, bounce off each other.

DR. PHIL PLAIT: Maybe the name is just wrong. Maybe they just call it a lightsaber. That doesn't mean it's made of light, if it's a force field that comes out and it's filled with a plasma or something like that.

"Forget your other organs—it's your brain you care about. You get a machine that lives forever, put your brain in the machine."

—DR. NEIL DEGRASSE TYSON, ASTRO-MAD SCIENTIST

StarTalk Live!: I, Robot (Part 2)

Will We Ever Be Able to Put a Human Brain in a Robot?

Bill Clinton, the 42nd president of the United States, talks about the future of robotics and medicine: "I keep meeting all these friends of mine that have two new hips and knees and all this . . . It looks like we're going to have replacement parts for just about everything. But if they replace your brain, would you still be you? Will there be the equivalent of like a SIM card or some sort of hard drive that takes everything out of your brain if you get a new one, and puts it back in the new brain?"

Well, Mr. President, the complexity of the brain far exceeds the storage capacity of any computer disk or card we have today. And the brain's synaptic structure changes so quickly that any digital backup of you probably wouldn't be you anymore in a matter of minutes—or even seconds. So go with a brain transplant rather than a brain backup. ■

TOUR GUIDE

Do Drones Follow Asimov's Laws of Robotics?

In Isaac Asimov's Robot novels, it is posited that humans have the wisdom to program robots not to harm humans, disobey humans, or destroy themselves, except under certain limiting conditions. The level of autonomous robotic ability that current military drones have—to plot a course to home base, for example, if a remote-control signal is lost—would not rise to the level of robotic intelligence expressed in Asimov's noble laws. If drones were to become that intelligent, who knows what they'll be programmed—or, on their own, decide—to do.

"Yeah, do you want to be buried, cremated, or uploaded? You get a choice."

—JASON SUDEIKIS, COMEDIAN

THINK ON THIS ▶ **Do Artificial Beings Have Human Rights?**

Brent Spiner, who played the android Data in *Star Trek: The Next Generation*, describes an episode that meant a lot to him: "[It] was an episode called 'The Measure of a Man,' in which my character was on trial, basically to decide whether or not he . . . was a sentient being . . . and whether, if he was not sentient, were we creating a race of slaves . . . or did he have his own right to his own existence?"

Artwork depicts events within specific cells of living tissue.

StarTalk Live!: Big Brains at BAM (Part 2)

Is Brainwashing Real?

Hypnotists are often shown with a swinging pocket watch.

Human brains—and thus people's behaviors and personalities—are malleable, as evidenced by radical terrorists and fanatic cults. Can that kind of control now be exerted with machines?

Neural prosthetics, such as cochlear implants for hearing or spinal cord stimulators for pain relief, are already widely used in human medicine. Amazingly, scientists using neural prosthetics can now control some rudimentary animal behaviors. Flying insects with electrodes in their brains can be commanded, for example, to turn left or right with a computer or joystick.

Optogenetics is another part of neuroscience, where parts of the brain are both scanned and stimulated using light signals. Optogenetic devices are aimed at communication—interpreting the brain's electrical signals and then sending messages back with light. Could memories and instructions be implanted as well? The implications for medicine—and possibly espionage—are staggering. ∎

`Cosmic Queries: A Stellar Sampling`

Can HAARP Manipulate the Weather?

From 1993 to 2015 the U.S. Air Force constructed and ran the High Frequency Active Auroral Research Program (HAARP), probing the ionosphere to see if radio signals could be enhanced in Earth's upper atmosphere to improve wireless communication or surveillance.

Rumors began to spread. Conspiracy theorists—including Venezuela's president at the time, Hugo Chávez—claimed HAARP was being used for nefarious tasks: shooting down an airplane, destroying the space shuttle *Columbia,* controlling minds, spreading disease, and creating storms, floods, earthquakes, and global warming. Even though it seems clear that these claims are false, a good scientist is willing to consider the evidence.

Here's Neil's reaction: "There are people who are sure that the government is stockpiling aliens and controlling everything about anything we would ever think about, and they clearly have never worked for the government . . . I have not been convinced by any of the reports to suggest that experiments in the upper atmosphere, physics experiments, are having any effect on our weather whatsoever." ■

BACK TO BASICS

How High Could a Kite Fly?

"The higher the kite goes, the more string is dangling beneath it. You reach a point where the weight of the string rivals the weight and updraft buoyancy of the kite . . . If you had a really huge kite, you could take it up to the stratosphere. The problem is, in the stratosphere, wind speeds are several hundred miles an hour." —Dr. Neil deGrasse Tyson, astro–Mary Poppins–ist

DID YOU KNOW

Research is being done on the possibility of flying windmill-like kites thousands of feet in the air to generate electricity from high-speed winds.

THINK ON THIS ▶ Does the Archimedes Mirror Attack Work?

According to legend, the ancient Greek inventor Archimedes set fire to invading Roman ships using bronze shields to focus sunlight. In 2005 Dr. David Wallace at MIT was able to simulate such an attack under controlled conditions. But when he and the hosts of TV's *MythBusters* tried it with 500 high school students on shore pointing big mirrors at a boat in the water, it didn't work.

An imagined future city on the coast

What Will Cities of the Future Be Like?

The gleaming spires and crisp lines of futuristic space cities have long been a mainstay of science fiction and its high-tech visionaries. They sometimes seem to be here already; just take a look from a distance at the skylines of New York, Shanghai, London, or Dubai. But dystopic visions of decaying urban wastelands have also been shown, perhaps most famously in the 1982 film *Blade Runner.* Can technology be used to stave off the ugly and send in the beautiful? If so, when?

"With a flying car, you're talking about going 3-D . . . But then you go to the street and suddenly you're two-dimensional . . . Have more car tunnels, [and you] alleviate congestion completely."

—ELON MUSK, TECH ENTREPRENEUR

"We have smart materials, adaptive structures," begins futurist Melissa Sterry's prediction. "We have entire buildings that can move. And we have the sensors, the information systems to inform those processes . . . The built environment is on the cusp of acknowledging, 'My God, we've actually got to get with the times. We've got to take advantage of these new opportunities' . . . We will have very smart cities by the year 2020 . . . The kind of bionic city I'm talking about, I'm giving a timeline of between 2040 and 2050." ■

Homer appeared as a robot in The Simpsons' "Days of Future Future" episode (2014).

A Conversation With Seth MacFarlane

Do Science, Sci-Fi, and Comedy Mix?

On Family Guy, *writer Seth MacFarlane often puts character Stewie in sci-fi situations.*

Many of us, sadly, know science only from humorless teachers and their classes. But in the right hands, science and comedy can be as tight as a tick on a tauntaun.

"I was always a big science-fiction fan, so I whenever possible jumped at the opportunity to have Stewie veer into that world," says *Family Guy* creator Seth MacFarlane. "Because certainly animation fans tend to be fans of science fiction and have an interest in science."

A few years back, psychologist Dr. Nina Strohminger published a scientific study with an earthshaking conclusion: "Farts make everything funnier." From speculations of Superman's destructive flatulence to discussions of astronauts shooting around the ISS, astro-silent-but-deadly-ist Dr. Neil deGrasse Tyson has compiled plenty of evidence to support Nina's claim. "But, just to be precise, that's exactly how the Shuttle lifts. It expels gas out of one end, and the physical shuttle recoils in the other." ∎

If In Space, No One Can Hear You Scream . . .

y did we hear explosions in *Gravity*? Movies don't have to be scientifica
accurate to be entertaining. *Star Wars*, one of the great sci-fi movie
franchises of all time, is fundamentally untrue to the laws of physics,
ut we like it anyway. How about closer-to-Earth movies, like *The Martiar*
Here are a few comments from Neil, many of them tweeted
right after he saw the movie.

||||||
◀ GRAVITATIONAL HAIRSTYLING

@neiltyson: "Mysteries of #Gravi
[Sandra] Bullock's hair, in otherw
vincing zero-G scenes, did not flo
on her head." Must be using reall
astronaut mousse.

TTER TOGETHER

yson: "Mysteries of #Gravity: When
e] Clooney releases Bullock's
he drifts away. In zero-G a single
gs them together." But then
s the drama in that?

||||||
◀ WHAT'S IN A TITLE

@neiltyson: "Mysteries of #Gravi
Bullock, a medical doctor, is serv
Hubble Space Telescope."
@neiltyson: "Mysteries of #Gravi
Astronaut Clooney informs medic
tor Bullock what happens medica
during oxygen deprivation."

◀ SAY IT AIN'T SO!

"Yes, absolutely, the sandstorm [in *The Martian*] is inaccurate . . . I just didn't care. I wanted a good reason to strand him there, and at the time I wrote it most people didn't know that." —Andy Weir, author of *The Martian*

||||||

▲ MARTIAN GARDENING

The Martian's greenhouse is full of potatoes? As long as there is enough water and grow lights, maybe. Essential soil nutrients for potato growth, though, are probably lacking, even with fertilizer.

||||||

 SPACE TRAVELERS

The rotating sections of *The Martian*'s spacecraft can indeed create acceleration that mimics gravity on a large spaceship. We still need some engineering innovations to make it possible, though.

||||||

▲ STAR POWER

@neiltyson: "In @StarWars #TheForceAwakens, if you were to suck all of a star's energy into your planet, your planet would vaporize." Bye-bye, Starkiller.

||||||

◀ SPACE VOLUME

@neiltyson: "In @StarWars #TheForceAwakens, the TIE fighters made exactly the same sound in the vacuum of space as in planetary atmospheres." Same goes for the X-wings and the Millennium Falcon.

"It's a very strong desire for humans to believe in things in the sky . . . And it's related to the whole concept of humans wanting to find meaning and purpose . . . UFOs fit this bill perfectly."
—MAJ. JAMES MCGAHA, ASTRONOMER AND FORMER USAF PILOT

CHAPTER FOUR

Could Bigfoot Be a Space Alien?

n a story arc of the classic 1970s show *The Six Million Dollar Man,* Bigfoot, also known as Sasquatch, is revealed to be a space alien—misunderstood and mistreated, but overall a really nice guy.

So that was a work of fiction. It wasn't real! Tell that to all the people who are sure they've seen a giant manlike creature wandering the woods with them. Will they believe you? How about the people who have seen UFOs and big-eyed extraterrestrials? The tricks our brains can play about what we think we've experienced can be complex and astonishing—and those are the same tricks other people exploit to befuddle us. Will their efforts defraud us or delight us? If we know what the tricks are, we can make a choice.

With the scientific confirmation of thousands of planets beyond our solar system and the near certainty of finding more, can finding aliens be far behind? Imagine what'll happen if we succeed.

A friendly meeting of Bigfoot and an extraterrestrial visitor

Who You Gonna Call to Bust Your Ghosts?

n 1998 British engineer and part-time psychic investigator Vic Tandy published a study showing that exposure to infrasound—sound waves below the threshold of human hearing—could cause eerie discomfort and possibly ghost-like visual hallucinations in people. Might further investigation of this sort of phenomenon be worthwhile?

> "If you're alive and then you're dead, and you're on a scale, your weight doesn't change . . . . As for a soul— if you want to believe there is one—there is no evidence that it has mass."
>
> —DR. NEIL DEGRASSE TYSON, ASTRO-SOUL-ICIST

Dan Aykroyd, actor and co-screenwriter of *Ghostbusters* thinks it is: "I want scientists to begin to inquire: What is the particulate matter? What is going on electrically? What's acting here? Is it oxygen? Nitrogen? What's in the air that can produce an apparition where people can actually manifest, in their vision, the apparition of someone who's dead? That's where I think spiritualism should go, right into the scientific. And so we've got to entice serious scientific inquirers to look into this. So far, no one is interested—except me." ∎

The battered cast of Ghostbusters *in 1984*

DID YOU KNOW

Around the year 1900, numerous scientists tried to take pictures of the human soul using x-rays, a newfangled technology at the time. It didn't work.

THINK ON THIS ▶ Is Hell Located Inside a Black Hole?

A few years ago, two televangelists on a U.S. TV broadcast claimed to show that black holes fulfill all the technical requirements of hell as described in the Bible. They were awarded an Ig Nobel Prize for their efforts. Inserting scientific ideas into religious contexts is hardly unique; another calculation was made, for example, showing that heaven must be hotter than hell. And in 1951, Pope Pius XII issued a papal encyclical declaring that the big bang is proof that God exists.

StarTalk Live! at Town Hall With Buzz Aldrin (Part 1)

How Do We Know We Landed on the Moon?

Hundreds of hours of video, thousands of photographs, tens of thousands of people who worked on the Apollo project, and millions of pages of documents are not sufficient evidence to convince some people that humans have walked on the Moon. "One really neat piece of evidence is to look at the video of Buzz running on the Moon and the video from the later flights and the movies, and watch the way the dust moves," author Andrew Chaikin tells us. "It's not like anything you've seen on Earth . . . and that's impossible to fake—and certainly was impossible to fake in the 1960s and '70s."

And how about talking to one of those humans who took a lunar stroll?

"You put your foot down, kick your foot, and here on Earth it just kind of moves stuff out in front," astronaut Dr. Buzz Aldrin says. "But on the Moon, you do that, and it goes out and it all forms in a semicircle. It really is different, because there's no air." ■

BACK TO BASICS

Why Are People Fascinated With Crystals?

With their unusual shapes, crisp edges, and flat planes, large mineral crystals form only under special geological conditions. Not surprisingly, some people imagine they may have supernatural properties—but even if they don't, they can still be beautiful. Astro-crystal-ist Dr. Neil deGrasse Tyson explains how crystals got their power:

"Crystals were the world's first transparent solid things. Think about that. Normally, you think of solid, and nothing goes through it. Now I've got a solid thing that light can pass through. That's an awesome thought, and there it is in nature. Crystals were valued simply because they were different, and they were transparent, and it's a natural part of human curiosity to pick up that which is different and bring it home."

A man adjusts a display at Kennedy Space Center, Florida.

"Those are the seeds of the birth of science: the fact that we are curious about some things that are different than others."
—DR. NEIL DEGRASSE TYSON

An imagined sinkhole in the Bermuda Triangle

YouTube: Neil deGrasse Tyson Explains the Bermuda Triangle

What's Going On in the Bermuda Triangle?

The pulp science-fiction magazine Amazing Stories *launched in 1926.*

The stretch of ocean between Bermuda, Puerto Rico, and Florida has been traveled extensively since the time of Christopher Columbus. It's a zone where warm and cold conditions can intersect, leading to storms and rough waters. Atlantic hurricanes track through all the time.

Even in modern times, human choices and bad seas can lead to tragedy. In 2015 an experienced freighter captain steered his ship, *El Faro,* from Florida toward Puerto Rico just as the powerful Category 4 Hurricane Joaquin was moving through the area. The ship began taking on water and then lost radio contact. *El Faro* was never seen again.

Statistically, however, there are no more shipwrecks or plane crashes in that region than would be expected, given the amount of traffic and weather there. Or as Neil puts it: "You ever notice there are never any missing trains? Trains never disappear." ■

The Out-of-This-World UFO Show

Is That a UFO or a Cloud?

There are thousands, maybe millions, of UFO sightings every year. Many of them are easily explained as helicopters, planes, or human spacecraft. (Yes, you can see the International Space Station from Earth, and it looks really funky.) Almost all of the rest of them are natural phenomena like bright planets (especially Venus), lightning and other weather events, meteors, or cloud formations. Why do people so readily interpret what they see as alien forms? Dr. Neil deGrasse Tyson, astro-cognitive-ist, has an answer: "What happens is, when you see something unfamiliar in the sky, the brain tries to understand it and come to terms with it.

"I think they've actually studied Earth and have concluded that there's no sign of intelligent life. What hubris it is to suggest that they would want to visit us in the first place."

—DR. NEIL DEGRASSE TYSON, ASTRO-HUMILITY-IST

It'll go overboard in doing so, and so what it doesn't understand, it connects the dots, it invents missing pieces, and so, when you try to judge what an object is, or you try to judge how big it is, your brain fills in the gaps."

One particular kind of lens-shaped cloud is often mistaken for a UFO—or, even better, interpreted as an artificially generated cloud designed to disguise a UFO. Standing lenticular clouds occur naturally, low in the atmosphere, usually hovering over a natural land obstacle like a mountain or ridgeline. They're naturally beautiful—and can look just like a fluffy alien flying saucer. ∎

Cosmic Queries: UFOs

Why Do Flying Saucers Spin?

Flying saucers are sometimes depicted—or purportedly observed—to be spinning as they fly. It's logical: Spinning creates acceleration toward an object's outer edge, which could mimic gravity as long as the passengers stood with their feet against the edge. But if they stood upright or sat facing forward, there'd be a lot of flying furniture and some dizzy aliens.

EUGENE MIRMAN: *Your problem is that the whole saucer spins, and that's what a fool would build.*

NEIL: *Those would be stupid aliens. If they managed to do that, it would be violating very well-tested laws of physics.*

Only a fraction of saucer-shaped UFO reports over the decades actually describe the saucers as rotating. Hollywood depictions aren't consistent either; for example, compare *The Day the Earth Stood Still* (1951) with *Earth vs. the Flying Saucers* (1956). As for the ones that do appear to spin, it could be an optical illusion or just a thin outer shell that's spinning while the interior remains still. ■

DID YOU KNOW

In the 1950s a Canadian company was contracted to develop a saucer-shaped aircraft for the U.S. Air Force. Project 1794 ended without success, but it did produce some valuable aviation technology.

TOUR GUIDE

Haven't We Already Been Visited?

Maybe aliens already came here—not to colonize or conquer but just to stop by, take a look, or get some work done, and then take off again.

If that's so, as the physicist Enrico Fermi asked, where are they? According to the Fermi paradox, there should be all kinds of extraterrestrial activity, and our astronomical searches should have found it by now—unless the aliens went to a lot of trouble to disguise their activities. But what would be the point?

THINK ON THIS ▶ Why Would Aliens Want to Come Here Anyhow?

ALAN ALDA, ACTOR: "These aliens are not going to come here, because the first thing they saw were our television programs . . . The first thing they heard was Orson Welles's radio show about the 'War of the Worlds' . . . They think the place is overrun by tourists already."

JOHN HODGMAN, COMEDIAN: "Think of the amount of energy and resources it would take to reach this planet. What would be gained?"

What Would Meeting Aliens Be Like?

H. G. Wells's The War of the Worlds *described fictional Martian attacks.*

From horrible destruction in movies like *Independence Day* to benevolent greetings in *Star Trek: First Contact,* alien meetings with humans have long been imagined based on either fearful or wishful thinking.

One voice on the side of caution comes from physicist Dr. Stephen Hawking, who said it might not go well for us humans—we may, he mused, wind up in the same position as the Native American population when Columbus arrived. "The fear factor that Stephen Hawking is expressing is more a fear of how he knows we would treat other people than it is from any actual knowledge of how actual aliens would treat us," Neil says.

If Hawking's concerns are legitimate, then humans may need to take precautions to make sure we're never detected. Maybe we'd need to encrypt our electronic transmissions and wireless communications—so that when they go into space, they seem like random radio noise. This, suggests former NSA contractor Edward Snowden, might be why we're missing out on alien communications. ■

DID YOU KNOW
A new scientific survey for extraterrestrial intelligence called Breakthrough Listen will, over the next decade, search one million stars in our Milky Way and one hundred galaxies beyond it for signs of alien life.

THINK ON THIS ▶ Was the "Wow!" Signal an Alien Message?

In the 1970s a researcher working on the search for extraterrestrial intelligence (SETI) noticed a brief radio signal that looked so much like a possible coherent message that he circled it on the printout and wrote, "Wow!" next to it. The signal has never been heard again. Was it random noise? Have the aliens stopped transmitting—or started disguising their broadcasts? If we don't find it again, we may never know.

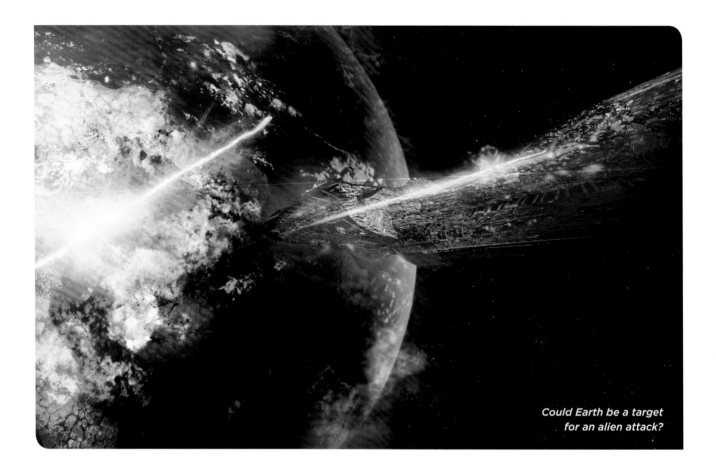

Could Earth be a target for an alien attack?

An Alien's Guide to Earth

Would Aliens Come to Save Us or Destroy Us?

NEIL: *When was the last time you walked by a pile of worms and said, "Gee, I wonder what they're thinking? I want to make peace with them."*

LYNNE KOPLITZ: *But I've also seen people stomp 'em, just because they were there.*

In our interactions with other living species, we eradicate them, domesticate them, love them, even worship them. Our behavior is often cultural: People in the U.S. raise cows to eat; people in India protect cows as sacred. So we can't imagine future human-alien interactions based on our current relations with other species alone.

"If aliens came to Earth across the galaxy, it means they've got more advanced technology than we do, so the fear factor makes us think they'll all be evil," Neil explains. "And what I think will save us is that they'll study Earth really hard, and they'll look at the species that calls itself dominant, and they will conclude, based on all the evidence that's available to them, that there is no sign of intelligent life on Earth, and thereby leave us alone." ■

Cosmic Queries: *Star Trek*

How Could the Klingons Have Become a Spacefaring Species?

DID YOU KNOW
Millions of 22nd- and 23rd-century Klingons didn't have forehead ridges, thanks to an epidemic caused in part by genetically engineered human DNA—and in part by inferior Hollywood costuming technology during the original *Star Trek* TV series.

Comedian and *Star Trek* geek Leighann Lord wonders: Given that the Klingon civilization of the *Star Trek* universe is all about combat, conquest, and glory, wouldn't they have destroyed themselves with advanced technology long before they even got off their home planet? Not necessarily, says Neil: "The culture of war is not inconsistent with the culture of technology. In fact, wars drive science. It's a pain to admit that, but it's true. The urge to survive creates extraordinary creative impulses in people to invent something that will make one person survive better than the other, and it's usually in the form of weaponry."

Think about it: We humans have the military technology to destroy our species, but we haven't done it. Maybe during their formative times, the Klingons had political and social restraints on their warlike tendencies as well. Or perhaps the Klingons could have developed their combative ways after they secured their path to the stars. ∎

Klingons in Star Trek III: The Search for Spock *(1984)*

*"I can imagine an alien species that is [just] energy . . .
The problem is, energy—it's hard to create form out of energy.
When energy becomes matter, you can make molecules and things . . .
Without it, it's amorphous, and it might be harder
to make amorphous life than material life."*
—DR. NEIL DEGRASSE TYSON, ASTRO-AMORPHO-CIST

"We are prisoners of the present, locked in the eternal transition between our past and our future."

—DR. NEIL DEGRASSE TYSON, ASTROPHYSICIST

CHAPTER FIVE

When Will We Be Able to Time-Travel?

This is the real frontier of science fiction. Sure, you can change the universe quite a bit with things like black holes and superpowers and star-killer planets. But if you can change the past, you can change *everything* about the universe in the blink of an eye—and nobody would even remember.

Could we go back in time—really manipulate time to that extent, regardless of what technological level we achieve? What exactly is time, anyway? If we think of time as Albert Einstein did—a dimension like length, width, or height, with its own special properties—then the bending of both space and time is in play. Warping and folding space might even allow us to break the fundamental limit of motion in the universe—the speed of light.

One thing is for sure: We can travel forward in time, no problem. We already know the science of how to stay young far into the future while the world ages around us. That's called time dilation—we just don't know how to do it yet. Time will tell.

Someday, time machines may bridge the past, present, and future.

YouTube: Neil deGrasse Tyson on Time:
Doctor Who, Star Trek, or Ray Bradbury?

What Is Time?

"Time is one of the most illusive aspects of physics," says cosmologist Dr. Janna Levin. "We almost imagine it spatially. We almost imagine it like a dimension. But I can't look forward in that dimension the way I can look left. And I can't turn around and look back in that dimension the way I can look right."

Albert Einstein explained in his general theory of relativity that time is a dimension, knit together with the three dimensions of space to create the four-dimensional flexible medium we call space-time. When you move in 4-D, your path is called a world line. Dr. Neil deGrasse Tyson, astro-time-icist, explains: "Other than that, [time] is a term in an equation that allows you to localize something on a world line. And a world line is where you are in space and where you are in time . . . You have never been at a place except for at a time. And you have never existed in a time except at a place. The two go together."

Sounds simple enough—with one important wrinkle. Whereas length, width, and height are bidirectional, time is unidirectional. So when you're measuring a four-dimensional distance in our universe—known as an interval of proper time—the time term has the opposite sign of the length, width, and height terms. That's what makes time travel seem so weird—and why moving backward in time is unphysical. ■

BIOGRAPHY

ᐁᐁ

Albert Einstein, Person of the 20th Century

Albert Einstein (1879–1955) got through school, earned his doctorate, and got a job, all without excelling but all well enough to give him the time and opportunity to do what he really wanted to do: think about challenging problems in physics. Then in a single "year of miracles," 1905, he described theories for three major scientific mysteries and deduced the formula $E = mc^2$. Einstein gained worldwide fame when his general theory of relativity was confirmed. Later in life, his contemplations of science, education, the cosmos, and human nature earned him the distinction as *Time* magazine's "Person of the Century."

"Astronauts age ever so slightly more slowly than you and I do . . . by being in orbit . . . When you're in a jet airplane flying around the world, your time is passing ever so slightly more slowly."

—BILL NYE THE TIME-DILATION GUY

THINK ON THIS ▶ Are There Places Where Time Passes Differently?

The rate of time passing changes from place to place all the time. The effects are tiny in our daily lives but definitely measurable with nanosecond precision. Faster-moving objects, for example, experience time more slowly than slower-moving objects. Gravity also slows you down; if you and a friend were both, say, hanging out near a black hole, the one closer to it would age more slowly.

DID YOU KNOW
Every second, a beam of light in the vacuum of space travels exactly 299,792,458 meters, or almost exactly 186,282 miles.

Sunlight travels to Earth in roughly eight minutes.

"When I wrote my science-fiction story, it was 'zero-point energy.' But that isn't as jazzy as gravitational waves . . . You get the gravitational wave in front of you to be a little lower than the one behind and you . . . whoosh!"

—DR. BUZZ ALDRIN, ASTRONAUT

Cosmic Queries: Time-Keeping

Does Time Ever Go Backward?

Probably not, although we don't know for sure. According to the mathematics of time dilation, exceeding the speed of light creates travel not in *negative* time, but rather *imaginary* time. "We know that there is this sort of clock," cosmologist Dr. Janna Levin says. "The clock never stops, we never turn around and go back. We can never accidentally go the wrong direction in time. It's always pushing us forward."

▶ WHAT ARE TACHYONS?

According to special relativity, only light can move at the speed of light—in our universe, everything else is slower. Particles that travel faster than light are called tachyons. If they exist, they might hold the key to time travel. As Neil puts it: "If I sent you a tachyon signal, you would get it before I sent it. We don't know if they exist, but it works on paper."

▶ HOW CAN WE PERFORM FASTER-THAN-LIGHT EXPERIMENTS?

Astro-boom-icist Dr. Neil deGrasse Tyson answers: "Light moves fastest in a vacuum. It travels a little slower going through air. It travels a little slower going through water . . . Even slower through glass . . . or diamond. Send a particle through there faster than that speed, [and] that will create . . . a mini light boom."

▶ COULD WE CATCH A GRAVITATIONAL WAVE?

Not to be confused with gravity waves, which happen on lakes and oceans, gravitational waves are ripples in space itself—length, width, and height. They're tiny, though, and only huge events—like exploding stars or colliding black holes—can generate them. So surfing on them might be a little tough. ■

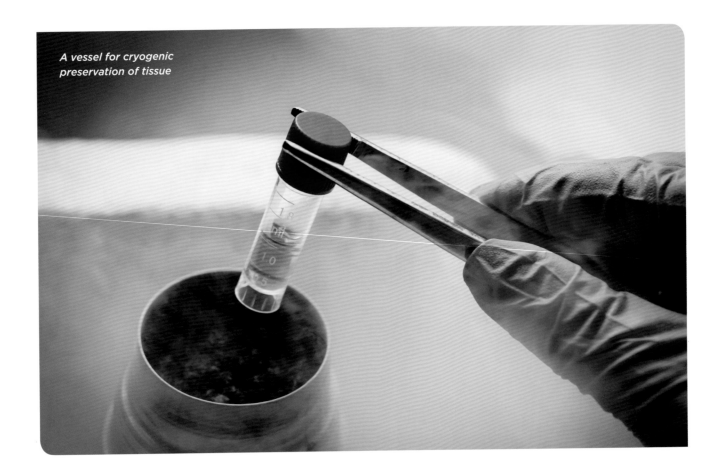

A vessel for cryogenic preservation of tissue

Did Walt Disney Get It Right With Cryogenics?

Walt Disney with Mickey Mouse

Urban legend has it that Walt Disney had his body frozen at the moment of his death. (Nope; he was cremated.) But would cryogenics be a way to travel into the future without aging? Human biological tissue is probably too fragile to survive being frozen for very long.

"You freeze the people, and they can wake up when they get to their destination," explains Dr. Phil Plait. "We don't know how to do that. You freeze somebody, they're frozen. That's bad . . . I suppose we can send [Disney's] head to Alpha Centauri and see what happens."

"Bad freezer burn, fellas," adds Leighann Lord.

Nevertheless, the idea of frozen human hibernation has been around a long time and exploited by lots of writers and filmmakers—including, ironically, the Walt Disney Studios. Several of the studio's recent superhero movies feature Captain America, who was accidentally frozen in 1945 and thawed out decades later. ■

There Are No Time Travelers—So Does Time Travel Even Exist?

Fraser Cain, the publisher of Universe Today, once asked Neil: "Doesn't the fact that there are no time travelers now prove that time travel will never be invented in the future?"

Neil's answer: "That's a pretty good argument . . . It might be that your time-travel machine can only take you into the future, and then you don't have these paradoxes of killing your grandmother, and then you're never born."

Time travel is a theme on *The Big Bang Theory.*

You could, of course, be exceptionally careful. In the television series *Star Trek: Voyager,* time travelers follow what they call the Temporal Prime Directive, sacrificing everything, including even their own existences, to preserve the time line.

In the short story "Ripples in the Dirac Sea" by NASA astrophysicist and award-winning writer Dr. Geoffrey Landis, a time traveler could not commit the "grandmother paradox," because every time he returned to the present, all the changes he'd caused to the past had disappeared. ■

BACK TO BASICS

Can You Travel Back in Time and Erase Yourself?

"Pick a time where two of your ancestors mated and produced one of your ancestors," proposes astro-pacifist Dr. Neil deGrasse Tyson. "All you have to do is prevent them from mating. You don't have to kill anybody." That works as long as only one time line exists in the universe. On the other hand, such a trip may in fact create an entirely new time line in which you would not exist—but which you also would not have to experience.

THINK ON THIS ▶ Does Time Travel Also Mean Space Travel?

Six months ago, because of its motion around the Sun, Earth was nearly 200 million miles from where it is now. So unless some sort of space-time relativity were preserved for time travel, in the way that a bird in flight doesn't shoot off into deep space, dizzying calculations would be required to land where you want. "You gotta specify location as well as time. Otherwise, you're hosed," Neil warns. "It's quite the ballet."

"The idea that we can bend space easier than we can bend ourselves seems, to me, backwards. But that's just the physicist in me. What do I know?"

—DR. CHARLES LIU, ASTROPHYSICIST

The Science of *Interstellar* With Christopher Nolan

Could We Fold Space for Travel?

Space-time is a structure mathematicians call a manifold—which, as its name suggests, could theoretically be folded or at least bent in many directions.

In the general theory of relativity, gravity is the curvature of space-time; so we'd just need to control a source of gravity large enough to bend space-time inward and then snap it back out again. But gravity travels only at the speed of light—so unless the fold is a permanent crease, the act of folding may not help you achieve faster-than-light travel.

"You could do something like warp drive by contracting space-time between two points, bringing them closer together, jumping across—you don't have to travel 400 light-years—and then you push it back out again. No big deal," says Dr. Janna Levin, cosmologist. ∎

Bending space-time would enable travel between two distant points.

CONVERSATION

Neil Confesses: "I Was Wrong About Warp Drive!"

NEIL: I'm thinking, they're warping space, just like I would warp paper.

DR. CHARLES LIU: That is so wrong, Neil.

NEIL: Tell me how the warp drive works.

DR. CHARLES LIU: The warp nacelles create a subspace field around the ship, which allows it to slide through ordinary space faster than light.

NEIL: So I was wrong ... I beg forgiveness.

"The warp factor is how fast you're able to slide through this subspace stuff."

—DR. CHARLES LIU, ASTROPHYSICIST

Cosmic Queries: Super Powers

Could We Use Black Holes or a TARDIS to Time-Travel?

DID YOU KNOW
If you travel to the black hole
Cygnus X-1 in a year, stay a year,
and then come back in a year, you
will have aged only three years, but
traveled 1,201 years into the future.

Black holes are fun mathematical constructs and real physical objects. If a black hole spins fast enough, the geometry of the black hole changes—the "point singularity" at the center becomes a ring, and a doughnut-shaped region forms in which an object can theoretically go at any speed—even exceeding the speed of light—and maybe even time-travel backward!

A totally fictional, but possibly more entertaining, way to time-travel with a black hole is to use it as a power source. In the *Doctor Who* television series, the space-and-time-hopping TARDIS vehicle is powered by the Eye of Harmony—a huge collapsing star frozen in time at the moment it was starting to form a black hole. But the entire amount of energy produced by such a stellar collapse—a Type II supernova—would still not be nearly enough to power everything a TARDIS can do. ■

"It turns out if you have a rotating black hole, there's a trajectory through it where you could possibly come out the other side before when you left."

—DR. NEIL DEGRASSE TYSON

The TARDIS transports the main character in Doctor Who *anywhere in time and space.*

THINK ON THIS ▶ Did *Contact* Get It Right?

In the 1997 movie *Contact,* the protagonist travels in a pod designed to alien specifications. During her journey, 18 hours of time pass while everyone watching her on the ground experiences just a second or two. If her trip had been relativistic—that is, she had been somehow sped up—the time-dilation effects should have been reversed. But hey, this is alien stuff—so who knows what technology they'd have, right?

YouTube: Neil deGrasse Tyson Discusses
Time Travel in *Interstellar*

Is Time Travel Possible Using a Fifth Dimension?

In Madeleine L'Engle's classic novel *A Wrinkle in Time*, the characters traveled rapidly through the fifth dimension. This neat trick allowed them to zoom around the universe, have adventures on strange planets, and still get home in time for dinner. We have no idea if this will ever happen for real, but Dr. Neil deGrasse Tyson, astro-tesser-ist, thinks it certainly could: "If you go to a higher dimension, it is not unrealistic to think that you step out of the time dimension and now you look at time as though we look at space . . . If your whole time line is laid out in front of you, then you have access to it and you can jump in at any point and relive it . . . What does it mean to jump into it and then change something if it's already there?" ∎

TOUR GUIDE

Can You Fly Into the Sun to Time-Travel?

In both the original *Star Trek* TV series and the movie *Star Trek IV: The Voyage Home*, the crew members of the *Enterprise* hurl themselves backward and forward through time by piloting their ship toward the Sun and using it as a gravitational slingshot. Could that work? "You cannot do what they did in the movie," Neil tells us. "So just nip that one in the bud. The only way you could do something like that is if you had vastly more powerful gravity than the Sun."

The fifth dimension in Interstellar *(2014) is predicated in real physics.*

"You can ask, 'When was I born?' Well, you were always born. 'When did I go to college?' You're always going to college. 'When did I die?' You're always dying."

—DR. NEIL DEGRASSE TYSON,
ON VIEWING YOUR TIME LINE
FROM A HIGHER DIMENSION

YouTube: Neil deGrasse Tyson on Wormholes and Time Travel

Could Wormholes Be Used to Travel Someday?

DID YOU KNOW
The term "wormhole" was never used in the original *Star Trek* TV series. It wasn't introduced until *Star Trek: The Motion Picture.*

Actor George Takei, who played Sulu on *Star Trek,* asked Neil for his thoughts on the ultimate transportation system through space and time. Here's what he had to say: "Wormholes? We're not going anywhere without them . . . but we don't have the command over space-time, matter, and energy yet to make one . . . Yeah, I don't see why [we won't get there eventually] . . . The day we can summon the energy of a galaxy, the mass of all the stars in the supercluster . . . I can imagine manipulating matter, energy—putting curved pockets within the fabric of space between you and your destination—and then the universe becomes a 'wormhole Swiss cheese' set of highways. And then you go wherever you want." ∎

"We don't wield enough power over energy in the universe to just create wormholes on a whim. If we harnessed all the energy produced in all the several hundred billion stars of the Milky Way galaxy, that would be enough."

—DR. NEIL DEGRASSE TYSON,
ASTRO-WHIM-SICIST

THINK ON THIS ▶ So When Will This All Come True?

George Takei asked Neil how many lifetimes it'll be before humans are able to sculpt wormhole highways into space-time. His answer: "I don't know if it's farther away than someone in 1900 saying, 'Oh, we'll never get to the Moon,' and then 69 years later we're leaving boot prints." Will we ever know? We do know this for sure: The questions we will have to answer are the ones we have yet to ask.

Acknowledgments

The heart and dedication of each member of *StarTalk*'s production team, past and present, is manifest in every show, and can be felt across all pages of this book.

The producers of *StarTalk* are further grateful to deputy editor Hilary Black at National Geographic Books for conjuring the idea of a *StarTalk* book and for assembling the dream team of associate editor Allyson Dickman, senior editor Susan Tyler Hitchcock, art director Sanaa Akkach, director of photography Susan S. Blair, photo editor Kristin Sladen, production editor Judith Klein, photo assistant Patrick Bagley, editorial assistant Moriah Petty, imaging technician Wendy Smith, associate designer Katie Olsen, and assistant designer Nicole Miller, who together wrangled such diverse content into a stunning visual expression of the show itself.

The soul of *StarTalk* lives within the banter, humor, and content of our shows, offered by our guests and by our studio experts. They're hewn from pop culture, politics, and academia, and we warmly recognize those who were referenced in these pages and who have shared their insights behind our microphones: Marc Abrahams, James Aguiar, Alan Alda, Buzz Aldrin, Neil Armstrong, David Attenborough, Dan Aykroyd, Hank Azaria, Heather Berlin, Mayim Bialik, Michael Ian Black, Cory Booker, Anthony Bourdain, Charles Bourland, Max Brooks, LeVar Burton, David Byrne, Fraser Cain, Jimmy Carter, Wyatt Cenac, Andrew Chaikin, Michael Che, Bill Clinton, Stephen Colbert, David Cope, Brian Cox, David Crosby, R. Walter Cunningham, Richard Dawkins, Peter Diamandis, His Holiness Gyalwang Drukpa, Ann Druyan, Christopher Emdin, Carter Emmart, Laurence Fishburne, Helen Fisher, Andrew Freedman, Jim Gaffigan, Laurie Garrett, Malcolm Gladwell, John Glenn, Stephen Gorevan, Temple Grandin, David Grinspoon, Josh Groban, GZA, Chris Hadfield, Maeve Higgins, John Hodgman, G. Scott Hubbard, Arianna Huffington, Jamie Hyneman, Penn Jillette, James Kakalios, Michio Kaku, Stephen Keil, Robert F. Kennedy, Jr., Lynne Koplitz, Mark Kurlansky, Roger Launias, Sally Le Page, Judith Lean, Janna Levin, Ian Lipkin, John Logsdon, Seth MacFarlane, Sandra Hall Magnus, Bill Maher, Amy Mainzer, the Rev. James R. Martin, Susana Martinez-Conde, Mike Massimino, Peter Max, James McGaha, Seth Meyers, Moby, Elon Musk, Marion Nestle, Nichelle Nichols, Miles O'Brien, John Oliver, Rebecca Oppenheimer, Yvonne Pendleton, Phil Plait, Carolyn Porco, Ainissa Ramirez, Alan Rickman, David Rind, Joan Rivers, Mary Roach, Joe Rogan, Cynthia Rosenzweig, Paul Rudd, Tess Russo, Jeffrey Ryan, Oliver Sacks, Cara Santa Maria, Susan Sarandon, Adam Savage, Dan Savage, Kristen Schaal, Andy Serkis, Seth Shostak, Mark Siddall, Jason Silva, Lee Silver, Jennifer Simonetti-Bryan, Steven Soter, Brent Spiner, Steven Squyres, Melissa Sterry, Jon Stewart, Biz Stone, Nina Strohminger, Jason Sudeikis, George Takei, Ian Tattersall, Travis Taylor, Clive Thompson, The Tweet of God, Shannon Walker, James Webster, Andy Weir, Ruth Westheimer, Wil Wheaton, Peter Whiteley, Larry Wilmore, Will Wright.

Neil deGrasse Tyson, Chuck Nice, and Jeff Jarvis on the set of StarTalk

StarTalk is filmed in front of a live audience in the American Museum of Natural History's Cullman Hall of the Universe in the Rose Center for the Earth and Space. Host Neil deGrasse Tyson is the Frederick P. Rose Director of the Hayden Planetarium.

Contributors

Neil deGrasse Tyson, *StarTalk* host, is a graduate of the prestigious Bronx High School of Science. He earned his B.A. in physics from Harvard and his Ph.D. in astrophysics from Columbia. He is the author of dozens of research papers and ten books—two of which became PBS *NOVA* specials. Neil is the recipient of 19 honorary doctoral degrees, and is host of *Cosmos: A SpaceTime Odyssey,* a 13-part series on the universe that aired on Fox and the National Geographic Channel. His late-night *StarTalk* program is the first television talk show on science, now appearing on the National Geographic Channel. He lives in New York City with his wife and two children.

Charles Liu, author, is an astrophysics professor at the City University of New York's College of Staten Island and an associate with the Hayden Planetarium and Department of Astrophysics at the American Museum of Natural History in New York. His research focuses on colliding galaxies, quasars, and the star formation history of the universe. He earned degrees from Harvard and the University of Arizona, and held postdoctoral positions at Kitt Peak National Observatory and Columbia. Together with co-authors Robert Irion and Dr. Neil deGrasse Tyson, he received the 2001 American Institute of Physics Science Writing Award for the book *One Universe: At Home in the Cosmos.* He is also the author of *The Handy Astronomy Answer Book,* now in its third edition. He and his wife, who is way smarter than he is, have three children, who are also way smarter than he is.

Jeffrey Lee Simons, editor, is the social media director of *StarTalk Radio.* When he's not busy engaging with the greatest fans in the universe, he's also a writer. He is the author of *Spirit in Realtime,* the first installment of his near-future virtual reality/ cyberpunk young adult science-fiction series. Simons is also the co-author of the cause-related marketing handbook *Making Money While Making a Difference,* with Dr. Richard Steckel, and the author of two works with noted artist Viktor Koen: *Lexicon: Words and Images of Strange* and *Toyphabet.* He has a B.A. in literature from Georgetown University. He lives in New Jersey with his wife, his daughter, and four cats.

Additional Contributors

Bill Nye, *StarTalk* host, holds a B.S. in mechanical engineering from Cornell University and worked as an engineer at Boeing before creating and hosting his Emmy Award–winning PBS/Discovery Channel show *Bill Nye the Science Guy.*

Eugene Mirman, *StarTalk* cohost, is a comedian and actor. He voices Gene on Fox's Emmy Award– winning animated series *Bob's Burgers* and has had two Comedy Central specials and five comedy albums. He lives in Brooklyn, New York.

Chuck Nice, *StarTalk* cohost, is an 18-year veteran of stand-up comedy, with a rich history in television and on radio. He is the host of *Buy Like a Mega Millionaire* on HGTV, *The Juice* on Veria Living, and *The Hot 10* on Centric.

Leighann Lord, *StarTalk* cohost, is a stand-up comedian named "The Most Thought Provoking Black Female Comic" by NYC Black Comedy. She is also a contributor to the Huffington Post and the author of several books, including *Leighann Lord's Dict Jokes,* volumes one and two.

Illustration Credits

Front cover: (Tyson), Miller Mobley/AUGUST; (pinwheel), Thanate Rooprasert/Shutterstock; (monster), redefine images/Shutterstock;(Saturn & satellites), John Foxx/Getty Images; (shuttle Endeavor), NASA; (glasses), luxxtek/Getty Images; (microscope), Vitaly Korovin/Shutterstock; (stethoscope), Edward Westmacott/Shutterstock; (Hubble telescope), NASA; (asteroids), Scott Tysick/Getty Images; (background), European Space Agency, NASA and Felix Mirabel (the French Atomic Energy Commission & the Institute for Astronomy and Space Physics/Conicet of Argentina); Back cover: (UP LE), SVF2/Getty Images; (UP RT), Eric Isselee/Shutterstock; (LO LE), Dmitry/Shutterstock; (LO RT), Giovanni Cancemi/Shutterstock.

Interior: 1, NASA/Corbis; 2-3, NASA/JPL-Caltech; 6, Fedorov Oleksiy/Shutterstock; 7, FOX via Getty Images; 8 (UP), Courtesy National Geographic Channels; 8 (LO), John A. Davis/Shutterstock; 9 (UP), NASA/Bill Ingalls; 9 (LO), JoeFotoSS/Shutterstock; 12-13, NASA, ESA, and the Hubble Heritage Team (STScI/AURA)—ESA/Hubble Collaboration; 15, NASA/JPL-Caltech; 16, Dmitry/Shutterstock; 17, YURI KOCHETKOV/epa/Corbis; 18 (UP), Photo Still(s) from Star Trek—Courtesy of CBS Television Studios; 18 (LO), Photo Still(s) from Star Trek—Courtesy of CBS Television Studios; 19 (UP LE), NASA; 19 (UP CTR), Mark Avino, National Air and Space Museum, Smithsonian Institution; 19 (UP RT), NASA; 19 (LO), Glove by Final Frontier Design, Photo by Virgil Calejesan; 20 (UP), NASA; 20 (LO), RIA Novosti/Science Source; 20-21 (Background), pixelparticle/Shutterstock; 21 (UP), NASA; 21 (CTR), Li junfeng—Imaginechina via AP Images; 21 (LO), NASA/Corbis; 22 (UP), Sebastien Micke/Paris Match via Getty Images; 22 (LO), Galen Rowell/Corbis; 23 (UP), NASA; 23 (CTR), NASA; 23 (LO), NASA; 24, FOX via Getty Images; 25 (UP), James O. Davies; 25 (LO), NASA/JPL/MSSS; 26, NASA; 27 (UP), Fabio Berti/Shutterstock; 27 (LO), NASA; 29, Elena Shashkina/Shutterstock; 30 (UP), bonchan/Shutterstock; 30 (LO), www.BillionPhotos.com/Shutterstock; 31 (UP), NASA; 31 (LO), NASA; 32 (UP LE), NASA; 32 (UP RT), National Air and Space Museum, Smithsonian Institution; 32 (CTR LE), Eric Long, National Air and Space Museum, Smithsonian Institution; 32 (CTR RT), SSPL/Getty Images; 32 (LO LE), NASA/Roger Ressmeyer/Corbis/VCG/Getty Images; 32 (LO RT), Stringer/AFP/Getty Images; 33 (UP LE), NASA; 33 (UP RT), molotok743/Shutterstock; 33 (CTR), NASA; 33 (LO LE), NASA/Gioia Massa; 33 (LO RT), Keith Homan/Shutterstock.com; 34 (UP), NASA/Terry W. Virts; 34 (LO LE), Lukas Gojda/Shutterstock; 34 (LO RT), Valentyn Volkov/Shutterstock; 35 (UP LE), Philippe Desnerck/Getty Images; 35 (LO LE), Bill O'Leary/*Washington Post*/Getty Images; 35 (RT-A), Courtesy Wrigley; 35 (RT-B), bestv/Shutterstock; 35 (RT-C), Chattanooga Bakery, Inc.; 35 (RT-D), iStock.com/jfmdesign; 36 (UP), Edward Kinsman/Science Source/Getty Images; 36 (LO), Hummy/Shutterstock; 37 (UP), Olga Nayashkova/Shutterstock; 37 (LO), Igor Stevanovic/Shutterstock; 39, Victor Habbick/Visuals Unlimited, Inc./Getty Images; 40 (UP), Laguna Design/Getty Images; 40 (LO), LungLee/Shutterstock.com; 41 (UP), Cosmos Studios/Fuzzy Door Productions/National Geographic/Six Point Harness/The Kobal Collection/Art Resource; 41 (LO), Lilly Lawrence/Getty Images; 42 (UP), Alain r/Wikimedia Commons (https://creativecommons.org/licenses/by-sa/2.5/legalcode); 42 (LO), Roman Sigaev/Shutterstock; 43 (UP), Peter Ginter/Getty Images; 43 (LO), ESA/Hubble & NASA (http://creativecommons.org/licenses/by/3.0/legalcode); 44 (UP), NASA, H.E. Bond and E. Nelan (Space Telescope Science Institute, Baltimore, Md.); M. Barstow and M. Burleigh (University of Leicester, U.K.); and J. B. Holberg (University of Arizona); 44 (LO), X-ray: NASA/CXC/ASU/J. Hester et al.; Optical: NASA/HST/ASU/J. Hester et al.; Radio: VLA/NRAO; 45 (UP), Mark Garlick/Science Photo Library/Getty Images; 45 (CTR), Ian Cuming/Getty Images; 45 (LO), NASA, ESA, D. Coe (NASA Jet Propulsion Laboratory/California Institute of Technology, and Space Telescope Science Institute), N. Benítez (Institute of Astrophysics of Andalucía, Spain), T. Broadhurst (University of the Basque Country, Spain), and H. Ford (Johns Hopkins University, USA) (http://creativecommons.org/licenses/by/3.0/legalcode); 47, NASA; 48 (UP), NASA/JPL-Caltech; 48 (UP-Portrait), Frederick M. Brown/Getty Images; 48 (LO), Josh Spradling/The Planetary Society; 48 (LO-Portrait), Larry Busacca/Getty Images; 49 (UP), NASA/JPL-Caltech; 49 (UP-Portrait), Cornell University; 49 (LO LE), NASA; 49 (LO LE-Portrait), Phil Mumford; 49 (LO RT), NASA/JPL-Caltech/MSSS; 49 (LO RT-Portrait), Alan Fischer; 50 (LE), NASA/Marshall Space Flight Center; 50 (RT), NASA; 51 (UP), Amblin/Dreamworks/WB/The Kobal Collection/James, David/Art Resource; 51 (LO), Nicescene/Shutterstock.com; 52 (UP), querbeet/Getty Images; 52 (LO), David Paul Morris/Getty Images; 53 (UP), Marina Sun/Shutterstock; 53 (LO), Victor Habbick/Shutterstock; 54 (UP), Charles Taylor/Shutterstock; 54 (LO), ifong/Shutterstock; 55 (UP), NASA/Ames/JPL-Caltech; 55 (LO), shiva3d/Shutterstock; 56, solarseven/Shutterstock; 57 (UP), Tappasan Phurisamrit/Shutterstock; 57 (LO), Joshua Sharp/Shutterstock; 59, NASA/JPL-Caltech; 60 (Pluto), NASA/JHUAPL/SwRI; 60-61, NASA/Ames/JPL-Caltech; 62 (UP), NASA/JPL/Space Science Institute; 62 (CTR), Don Davis/NASA; 62 (LO), Courtesy of http://tabbythis.com; 63, John White Photos/Alamy Stock Photo; 64 (UP), NASA/JPL-Caltech; 64 (LO), ESA 2010 MPS for OSIRIS Team MPS/UPD/LAM/IAA/RSSD/INTA/UPM/DASP/IDA; 65 (UP), igor.stevanovic/Shutterstock; 65 (CTR), G10ck/Shutterstock; 65 (LO), givaga/Shutterstock; 66 (UP LE), Gary Ombler/Getty Images; 66 (UP RT), NASA/JHUAPL/SwRI; 66 (CTR), NASA/JPL-Caltech/UCLA/MPS/DLR/IDA; 66 (LO), Thomas Heaton/Getty Images; 67 (UP), NASA/JPL-Caltech; 67 (CTR), NASA/JPL; 67 (LO), Dennis di Cicco/Corbis; 68, J Foster/Getty Images; 69 (UP), NASA/JPL-Caltech/UCLA; 69 (LO), zhangyouyang/Shutterstock; 70-71, ESA/NASA; 73, wragg/Getty Images; 74 (UP LE), NASA; 74 (UP RT), Earth Science and Remote Sensing Unit, NASA Johnson Space Center (http://eol.jsc.nasa.gov/); 74 (LO), NASA/JPL-Caltech/SSI; 75 (UP), NASA; 75 (CTR), NASA/JPL; 75 (LO), Scott Kelly/NASA; 76, NASA; 77 (UP), Mickey Adair/Michael Ochs Archives/Getty Images; 77 (LO), NASA/JPL-Caltech/SSI; 78 (UP), Detlev van Ravenswaay/Science Source; 78 (LO), David A. Hardy/Science Source; 79, David Lees/Corbis; 80 (UP), Matt Cardy/Getty Images; 80 (LO), Claudio Divizia/Shutterstock; 81 (UP), James D. Balog; 81 (LO), bikeriderlondon/Shutterstock; 82 (UP), Henning Dalhoff/SPL/Getty Images; 82 (LO), Kichigin/Shutterstock; 83 (UP), aodaodaodaod/Shutterstock; 83 (CTR LE), Stephen Alvarez/National Geographic Creative; 83 (CTR), Nicolle Rager-Fuller, NSF; 83 (CTR RT), David A. Hardy/Science Source; 83 (LO), luxxtek/Getty Images; 84 (UP), NASA/JPL/University of Arizona; 84 (LO), © 2005 Mattias Malmer, from NASA/JPL data; 85 (UP), Valerio Pardi/Shutterstock; 85 (LO), Dmitriy Sivukha/Shutterstock; 86 (UP), De Agostini Picture Library/Getty Images; 86 (CTR LE), Michael Maslan Historic Photographs/Corbis; 86 (CTR RT), Babak Tafreshi/National Geographic Creative; 86 (LO LE), Bettmann/Corbis via Getty Images; 86 (LO RT), Roger Ressmeyer/Corbis/VCG/Getty Images; 87 (UP LE), David Parker/Science Source; 87 (UP RT), Richard Wainscoat/Alamy Stock

Photo; 87 (CTR LE), NASA; 87 (CTR RT), NASA/CXC/SAO; 87 (LO LE), NASA/Kepler mission/Wendy Stenzel; 87 (LO RT), Northrop Grumman; 89, Jan Cobb Photography Ltd./Getty Images; 90 (UP), James P. Blair/National Geographic Creative; 90 (LO), Yuri Samsonov/Shutterstock; 91 (UP), Rastan/Getty Images; 91 (LO), ESA/Rosetta/NAVCAM (http://creativecommons.org/licenses/by-sa/3.0/igo/legalcode); 92 (UP), Tim Wetherell—Australian National University (https://creativecommons.org/licenses/by-sa/3.0/deed.en); 92 (CTR), NASA, Philip James (University of Toledo), Steven Lee (University of Colorado); 92 (LO), MLiberra/Getty Images; 93, Zia Soleil/Getty Images; 94 (UP), Pictorial/Shutterstock; 94 (CTR), Pakhnyushchy/Shutterstock; 94 (LO), jerbarber/Getty Images; 95 (UP), Kuttelvaserova Stuchelova/Shutterstock; 95 (CTR), stjepann/Shutterstock; 95 (LO), Dmitry Molchanov/Shutterstock; 96 (UP), Charles D. Winters/Science Source; 96 (LO), Andrew Toth/Getty Images; 97 (UP), Alexander Fomchenko/Shutterstock; 97 (LO), Devonyu/Getty Images; 98 (LE), B Brown/Shutterstock; 98 (RT), Peezaar/Shutterstock; 99 (UP), nostal6ie/Shutterstock; 99 (CTR LE), Christopher Halloran/Shutterstock; 99 (CTR RT), IanRedding/Shutterstock; 99 (LO), aastock/Shutterstock; 101, Robin Houde photography/Getty Images; 102 (UP), Igor Sokolov (breeze)/Shutterstock; 102 (LO), Ryan McGinnis/Alamy Stock Photo; 103 (UP), Irwin Thompson/Dallas Morning News/Corbis; 103 (CTR), adike/Shutterstock; 103 (LO), Harvepino/Shutterstock; 104, trekandshoot/Shutterstock; 105, iStock.com/fightbegin; 106 (UP), Pal Szilagyi-Palko/Demotix/Corbis; 106 (LO), NASA/SDO/AIA/HMI/Goddard Space Flight Center; 107, Eric Phillips/Hedgehog House/Minden Pictures/National Geographic Creative; 108 (UP), Biophoto Associates/Science Source, colorization by Mary Martin; 108 (LO), Karen Kasmauski/Science Faction/Getty Images; 108 (RT), Kallista Images/Visuals Unlimited/Corbis; 109 (UP), Pyty/Shutterstock; 109 (CTR LE), Andrii Zhezhera/Shutterstock; 109 (CTR RT), Dumitrescu Ciprian-Florin/Shutterstock; 109 (LO), Enrico Bortoluzzi/Shutterstock; 110 (UP), Natalia D./Shutterstock; 110 (LO), TijanaM/Shutterstock; 111, Nick Kaloterakis/National Geographic Creative; 113, Derek Bacon/Ikon Images/Corbis; 114, Kostyantyn Ivanyshen/Stocktrek Images/Getty Images; 115 (UP), NASA/JPL-Caltech; 115 (LO), Kris Krüg/Getty Images; 116 (UP), iStock.com/AMR_Photos; 116 (LO), Jan Martin Will/Shutterstock; 117 (UP), STILLFX/Shutterstock; 117 (LO), Creativ Studio Heinemann/Getty Images; 118 (UP), AP Images/Gregorio Borgia; 118 (CTR), hidesy/Shutterstock; 118 (LO), Marcelo Horn/Getty Images; 119, Thanate Rooprasert/Shutterstock; 121, Johan Swanepoel/Shutterstock; 122 (UP), Alex Hubenov/Shutterstock; 122 (CTR), Eugene Ivanov/Shutterstock; 122 (LO), AP Images/APTV; 123 (UP LE), Will Crocker/Getty Images; 123 (UP RT), NASA; 123 (CTR), T photography/Shutterstock; 123 (LO LE), AZSTARMAN/Shutterstock; 123 (LO RT), KarSol/Shutterstock; 124, design56/Getty Images; 125 (UP), stuartbur/Getty Images; 125 (LO), Getty Images/Handout; 126 (UP), photo5963_shutter/Shutterstock; 126 (CTR), Hurst Photo/Shutterstock; 126 (LO), Yury Dmitrienko/Shutterstock; 127, Stocktrek Images/Getty Images; 128 (UP), Elena Schweitzer/Shutterstock; 128 (LO), Julien Tromeut/Shutterstock; 129 (UP), AP Images/Seth Wenig; 129 (LO), adike/Shutterstock; 130 (UP), redefine images/Shutterstock; 130 (LO), Monica Schipper/Getty Images; 131 (UP), Andrew Brusso/Corbis; 131 (LO), NASA/SDO/AIA; 132-3, vuk8691/Getty Images; 135, vicuschka/Getty Images; 136 (UP), Anna Hoychuk/Shutterstock; 136 (LO), ClarkandCompany/Getty Images; 137 (UP LE), O. Louis Mazzatenta/National Geographic Creative; 137 (UP RT), dionisvero/Getty Images; 137 (LO), marius-s/Getty Images; 138 (UP), urbanbuzz/Shutterstock.com; 138 (LO), BrianAJackson/Getty Images; 139, orcearo/Getty Images; 140 (UP), Africa Studio/Shutterstock; 140 (LO), Darrickphoto/Getty Images; 141 (UP), James Devaney/WireImage/Getty Images; 141 (LO), photosync/Shutterstock; 143, Angela Waye/Shutterstock; 144 (UP), Sophie Jacopin/Science Source; 144 (LO), Lars Niki/Corbis via Getty Images; 145 (LE), Grafissimo/Getty Images; 145 (UP RT), David Paul Morris/Getty Images; 145 (CTR RT), drserg/Shutterstock.com; 145 (LO RT), Frank Hoensch/Getty Images; 146 (UP LE), John Lamparski/WireImage/Getty Images; 146 (UP RT), Chance Yeh/Getty Images; 146 (LO LE), Ovidiu Hrubaru/Shutterstock.com; 146 (LO RT), Tim Mosenfelder/FilmMagic/Getty Images; 147 (UP LE), Helga Esteb/Shutterstock.com; 147 (UP CTR), Helga Esteb/Shutterstock.com; 147 (UP RT), Helga Esteb/Shutterstock.com; 147 (LO), JStone/Shutterstock.com; 148 (UP), iStock.com/Franck Boston; 148 (LO), WENN Ltd/Alamy Stock Photo; 149 (UP), PacoRomero/Getty Images; 149 (CTR), Neil deGrasse Tyson; 149 (LO), Helga Esteb/Shutterstock.com; 151, Marcus/marcusmphoto.com/Getty Images; 152 (UP), Africa Studio/Shutterstock; 152 (LO), Scanrail1/Shutterstock; 153 (UP), Robert Wallis/Corbis via Getty Images; 153 (LO), Dean Bertoncelj/Shutterstock.com; 154 (UP), alexaranda/Getty Images; 154 (LO), pekour/Getty Images; 155, Alija/Getty Images; 156 (UP), Daniel Huerlimann-BEELDE/Shutterstock.com; 156 (LO), Science Picture Company/Corbis; 157, iStock.com/Thomas Saupe; 158 (UP), Andrew Rich/Getty Images; 158 (LO), iStock.com/patty_c; 159, AF archive/Alamy Stock Photo; 161, GYRO PHOTOGRAPHY/amanaimagesRF/Getty Images; 162 (UP), REUTERS/Suzanne Plunkett; 162 (LO), mdmworks/Getty Images; 163 (Bacteria), xrender/Getty Images; 163 (Mustard Grass), EnlightenedMedia/Getty Images; 163 (Roundworm), Marcel Jancovic/Shutterstock; 163 (Fruit Fly), Roblan/Shutterstock; 163 (Banana), Maks Narodenko/Shutterstock; 163 (Zebra Fish), Mirko Rosenau/Shutterstock; 163 (Gorilla), Roman Samokhin/Shutterstock; 163 (Orangutan), Odua Images/Shutterstock; 163 (Chimpanzee), GlobalP/Getty Images; 163 (Darwin), The Print Collector/Getty Images; 164 (UP), stock_colors/Getty Images; 164 (CTR LE), Paul Zahl/National Geographic Creative; 164 (CTR RT), ArchMan/Shutterstock; 164 (LO LE), Lynn Bystrom/Getty Images; 164 (LO RT), fotojagodka/Getty Images; 165 (UP), Ivaschenka Roman/Shutterstock; 165 (CTR LE), jaroslava V/Shutterstock; 165 (CTR RT), Joe McNally; 165 (LO LE), GlobalP/Getty Images; 165 (LO RT), Portra/Getty Images; 166-7, diversepixel/Shutterstock; 169, van Bliznetsov/Getty Images; 170 (UP), Bernard Gotfryd/Getty Images; 170 (LO), Dmitri Ma/Shutterstock; 171 (UP), Floortje/Getty Images; 171 (LO), shunfa Teh/Shutterstock; 172 (UP), inhauscreative/Getty Images; 172 (LO), Centers for Disease Control and Prevention; 173 (UP), NIAID (https://creativecommons.org/licenses/by/2.0/legalcode); 173 (LO), Olena_T/Getty Images; 174 (UP LE), National Institute of Allergy and Infectious Diseases (NIAID); 174 (UP RT), Centers for Disease Control and Prevention/Dr. Mae Melvin; 174 (LO), Pictorial Press Ltd/Alamy Stock Photo; 175 (UP LE), Centers for Disease Control and Prevention/James Gathany; 175 (UP RT), Benedicte Desrus/Alamy Stock Photo; 175 (LO LE), Paula Bronstein/Getty Images; 175 (LO RT), Chones/Shutterstock; 176 (UP), Floortje/Getty Images; 176 (LO), Getty Images; 177, vitstudio/Shutterstock; 179, vchal/Getty Images; 180, Ploychan Lompong/Shutterstock.com; 181 (UP), Disney XD/ABC/Getty Images; 181 (CTR), AF archive/Alamy Stock Photo; 181 (LO), AF archive/Alamy Stock Photo; 182 (UP), iStock.com/Catherine Lane; 182 (LO), Getty Images; 183 (UP), AF archive/Alamy Stock Photo; 183 (LO), iStock.com/Jacob VanHouten; 184, AF archive/Alamy Stock Photo; 185 (UP LE), Martin Kemp/Shutterstock; 185 (UP RT), AF archive/Alamy Stock Photo; 185 (LO), welcomia/Shutterstock; 186 (UP LE), From: "Action Comics" #14 © DC Comics; 186 (UP RT), Bob Orsillo/Shutterstock; 186 (LO), Pictorial Press Ltd/Alamy Stock Photo; 187 (UP LE), CBS via Getty Images; 187 (UP RT), NASA/JPL-Caltech/2MASS; 187 (LO), AF archive/Alamy Stock Photo; 189, C.J. Burton/Corbis Collection/Getty

Images; 190, alengo/Getty Images; 191 (UP), CBS Photo Archive/Getty Images; 191 (LO), Alexey Kamenskiy/Shutterstock; 192 (UP LE), DSGpro/Getty Images; 192 (UP RT - Cox), Bob Lee/flickr (https://creativecommons.org/licenses/by/2.0/legalcode); 192 (UP RT - Tyson), Debby Wong/Shutterstock; 192 (LO), Rex Features via AP Images; 193 (UP), iStock.com/marekuliasz; 193 (CTR), Giovanni Cancemi/Shutterstock; 193 (LO), AF archive/Alamy Stock Photo; 194 (UP), Henning Dalhoff/Science Photo Library/Getty Images; 194 (LO), Brian A Jackson/Shutterstock; 195 (UP), Vivian Fung/Shutterstock; 195 (CTR), Tashatuvango/Shutterstock; 195 (LO), Granger, NYC — All rights reserved; 196, iurii/Shutterstock; 197 (UP), FOX via Getty Images; 197 (LO), FOX via Getty Images; 198 (UP), Moviestore Collection Ltd/Alamy Stock Photo; 198 (CTR), Pictorial Press Ltd/Alamy Stock Photo; 198 (LO), Moviestore Collection Ltd/Alamy Stock Photo; 199 (UP LE), ZUMA Press, Inc./Alamy Stock Photo; 199 (UP RT), ZUMA Press, Inc./Alamy Stock Photo; 199 (CTR LE), ZUMA Press, Inc./Alamy Stock Photo; 199 (CTR RT), Moviestore Collection Ltd/Alamy Stock Photo; 199 (LO), Moviestore Collection Ltd/Alamy Stock Photo; 201, Dale O'Dell/Alamy Stock Photo; 202 (UP), AF archive/Alamy Stock Photo; 202 (LO), Anna Bogatirewa/Shutterstock; 203 (UP), J. Palys/

Shutterstock; 203 (LO), Richard Barnes; 204 (UP), Victor Habbick Visions/Science Photo Library/Getty Images; 204 (LO), Mary Evans Picture Library/Alamy Stock Photo; 205, pixhook/Getty Images; 206 (UP), lazyllama/Shutterstock; 206 (CTR), Maria Toutoudaki/Getty Images; 206 (LO), lassedesignen/Shutterstock; 207 (UP), Mary Evans Picture Library/Alamy Stock Photo; 207 (LO), Copyright © 1997-2010 Big Ear Radio Observatory and North American AstroPhysical Observatory; 208, gremlin/Getty Images; 209, AF archive/Alamy Stock Photo; 211, Ryan J. Lane/Getty Images; 212 (UP), Jean-Leon Huens/National Geographic Creative; 212 (LO), koosen/Getty Images; 213, mitakag/Getty Images; 214 (UP), Olena Pavlovich/Getty Images; 214 (LO), dieKleinert/Alamy Stock Photo; 215 (UP), Aldo Murillo/Getty Images; 215 (CTR), Neil Jacobs/CBS via Getty Images; 215 (LO), agsandrew/Shutterstock; 216 (LE), Eugen Dobric/Getty Images; 216 (RT-Liu), National Geographic Channel; 216 (RT-Tyson), Debby Wong/Shutterstock; 217 (UP), iStock.com/Brendan Hunter; 217 (LO), AF archive/Alamy Stock Photo; 218 (UP), ESA/NASA/SOHO; 218 (LO), Moviestore Collection Ltd/Alamy Stock Photo; 219 (LE), Koya979/Shutterstock; 219 (RT), Talaj/Getty Images; 220, National Geographic Channel/Scott Gries.

Since 1888, the National Geographic Society has funded more than 12,000 research, exploration, and preservation projects around the world. National Geographic Partners distributes a portion of the funds it receives from your purchase to National Geographic Society to support programs including the conservation of animals and their habitats.

National Geographic Partners
1145 17th Street NW
Washington, DC 20036-4688 USA

Become a member of National Geographic and activate your benefits today at natgeo.com/jointoday.

For information about special discounts for bulk purchases, please contact National Geographic Books Special Sales: specialsales@natgeo.com

For rights or permissions inquiries, please contact National Geographic Books Subsidiary Rights: bookrights@natgeo.com

Printed in China

17/RRDS/1

Copyright © 2017 Curved Light Productions, LLC. All rights reserved. Reproduction of the whole or any part of the contents without written permission from the publisher is prohibited.

NATIONAL GEOGRAPHIC and Yellow Border Design are trademarks of the National Geographic Society, used under license.

ISBN Trade edition: 978-1-4263-3087-2
ISBN RLB edition: 978-1-4263-3088-9

The Library of Congress cataloged the original edition as follows:
Names: Tyson, Neil deGrasse. | Liu, Charles, 1968 April 5- | Simons, Jeffrey Lee.
Title: Startalk : everything you ever need to know about space travel, sci-fi, the human race, the universe, and beyond / with Neil deGrasse Tyson.
Other titles: Star talk
Description: Washington, D.C. : National Geographic, 2016. | Contributing editors, Charles Liu, astrophysics professor at the City University of New York's College of Staten Island, and Jeffrey Lee Simons, social media director of StarTalk Radio.
Identifiers: LCCN 2016019357 | ISBN 9781426217272 (hardcover : alk. paper)
Subjects: LCSH: Cosmology--Popular works. | Outer space--Exploration--Popular works. | Earth sciences--Popular works. | Human beings--Popular works. | Science fiction--Social aspects.
Classification: LCC QB982 .S74 2016 | DDC 523.1--dc23
LC record available at https://lccn.loc.gov/2016019357